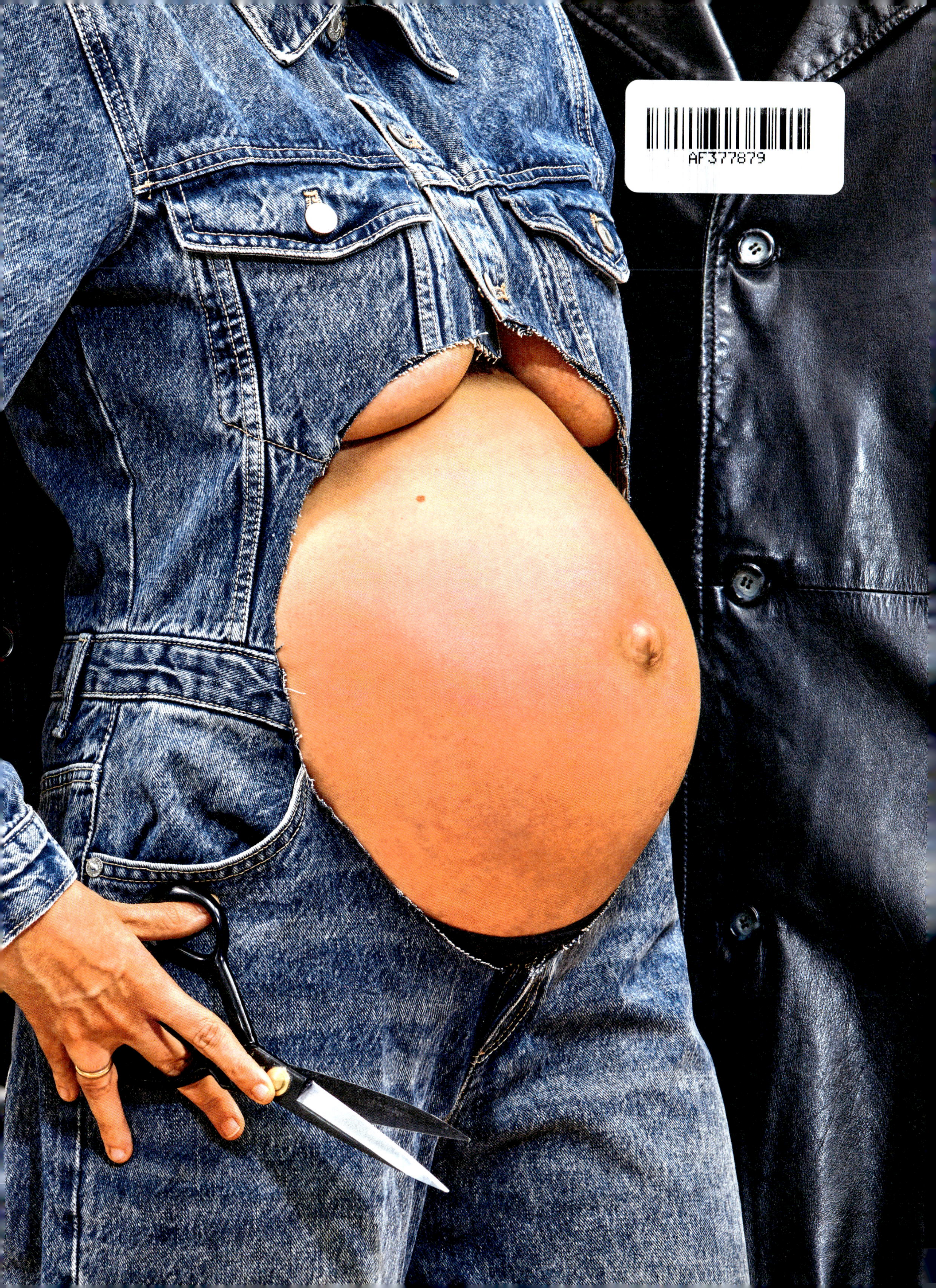
AF377879

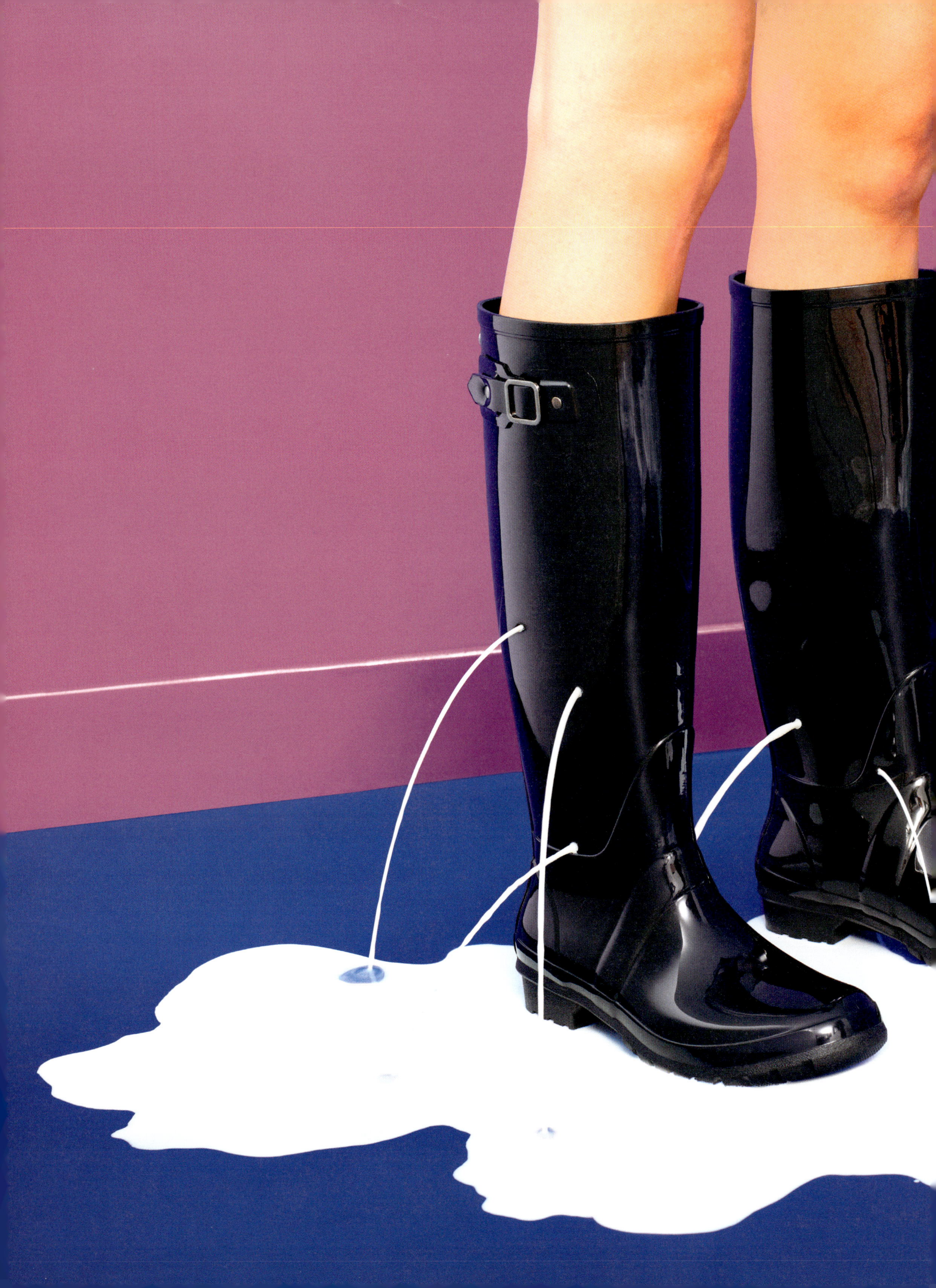

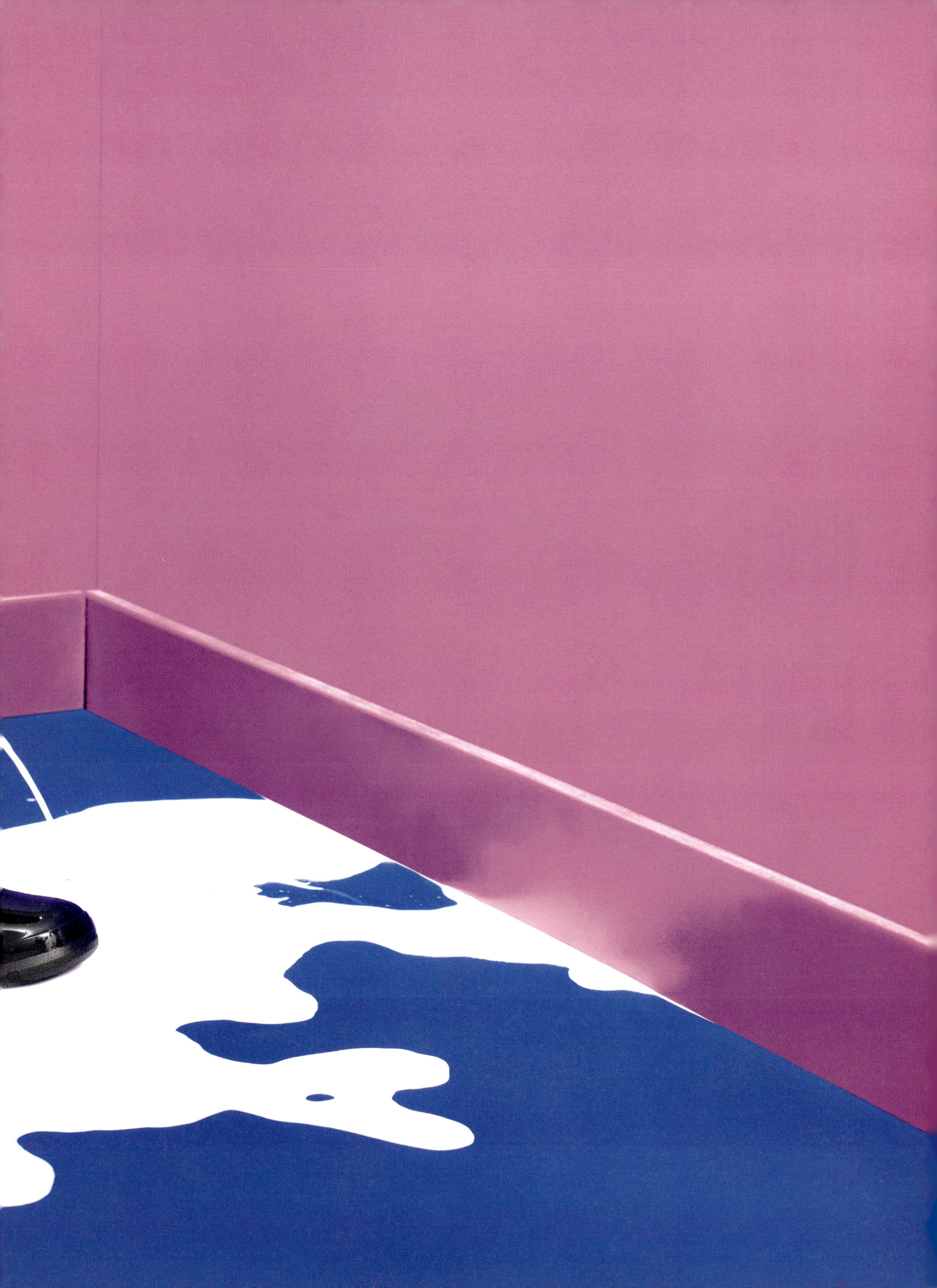

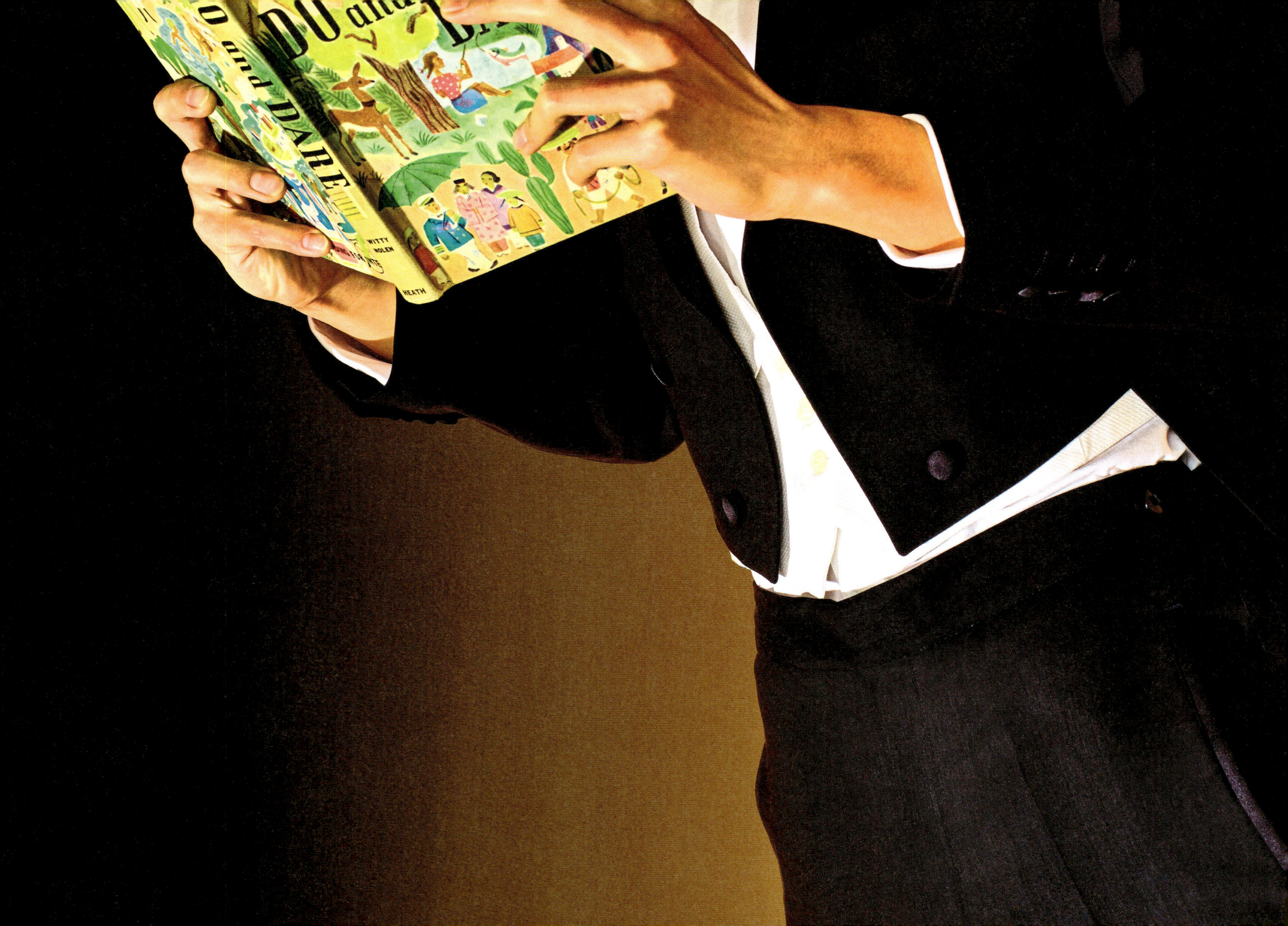
DO and DARE
WITTY
NOLEN
HEATH

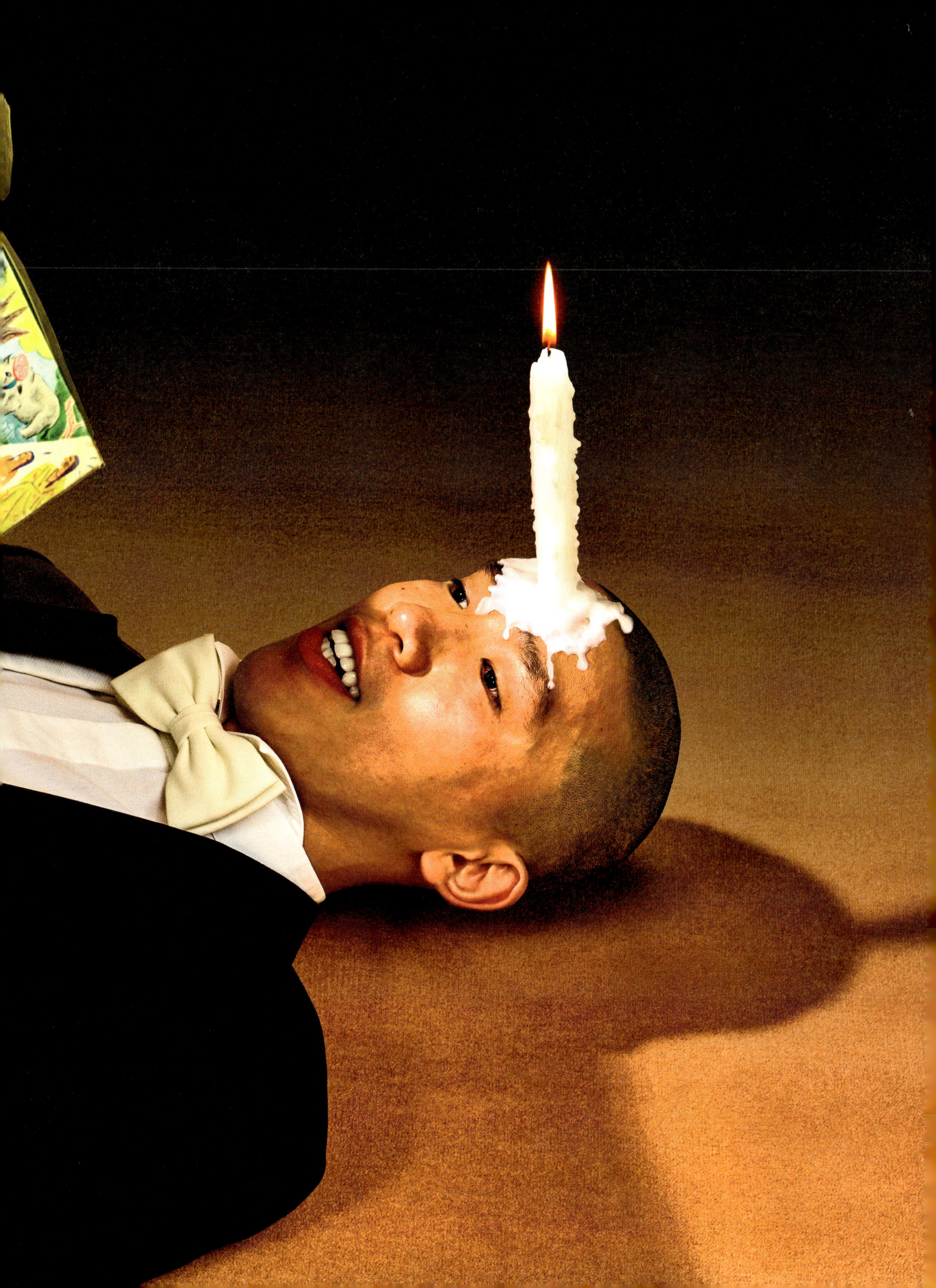

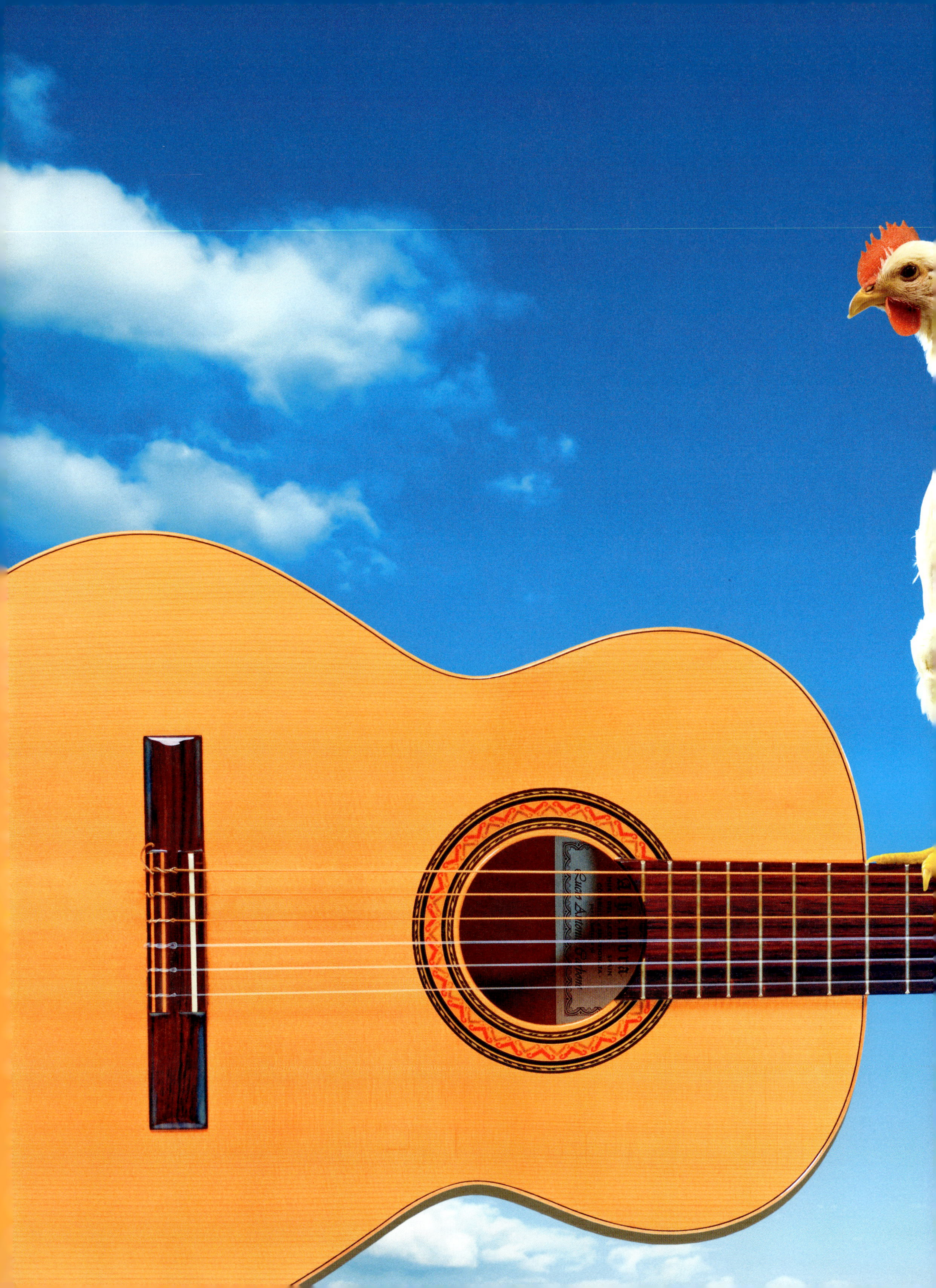

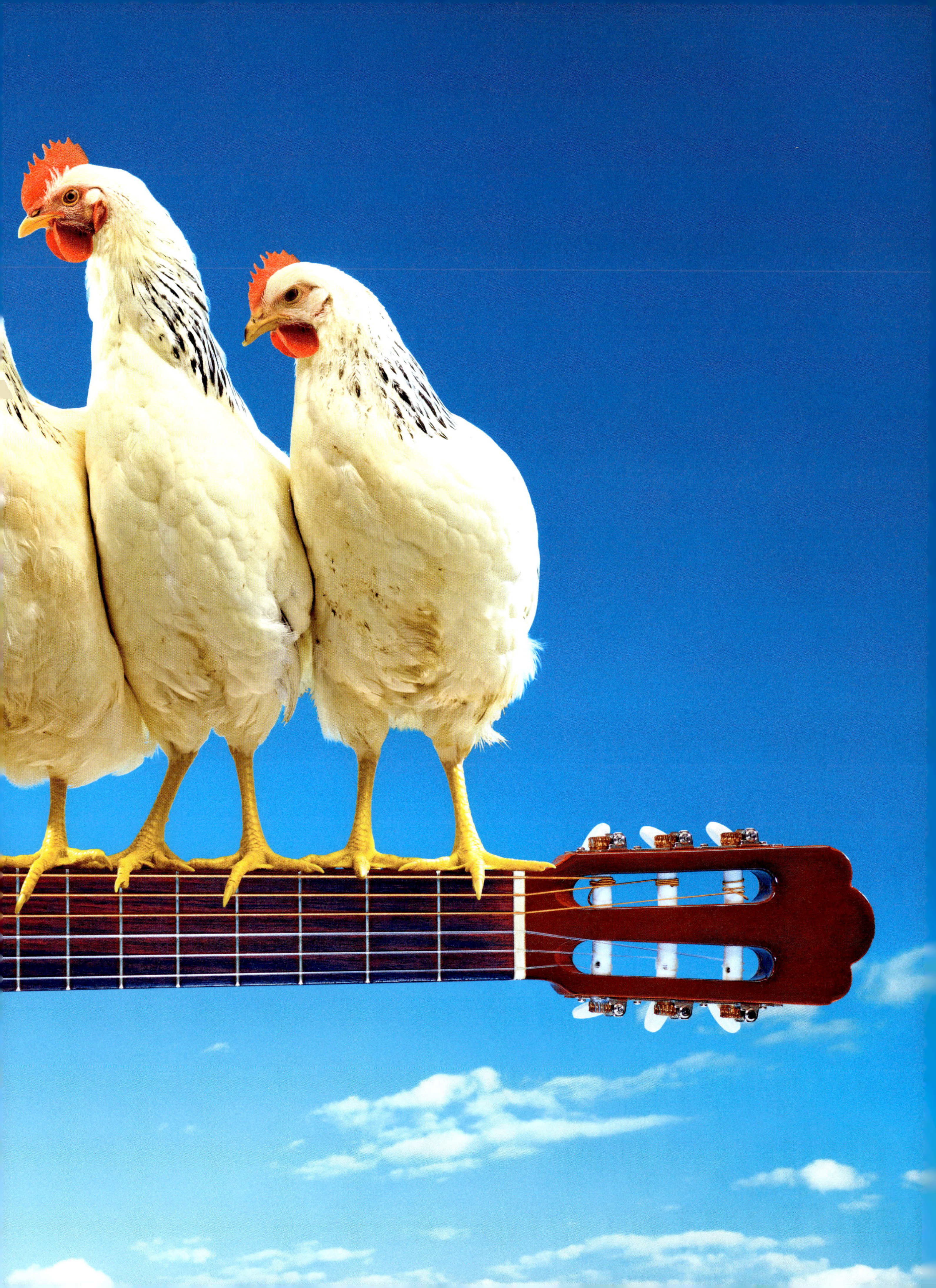

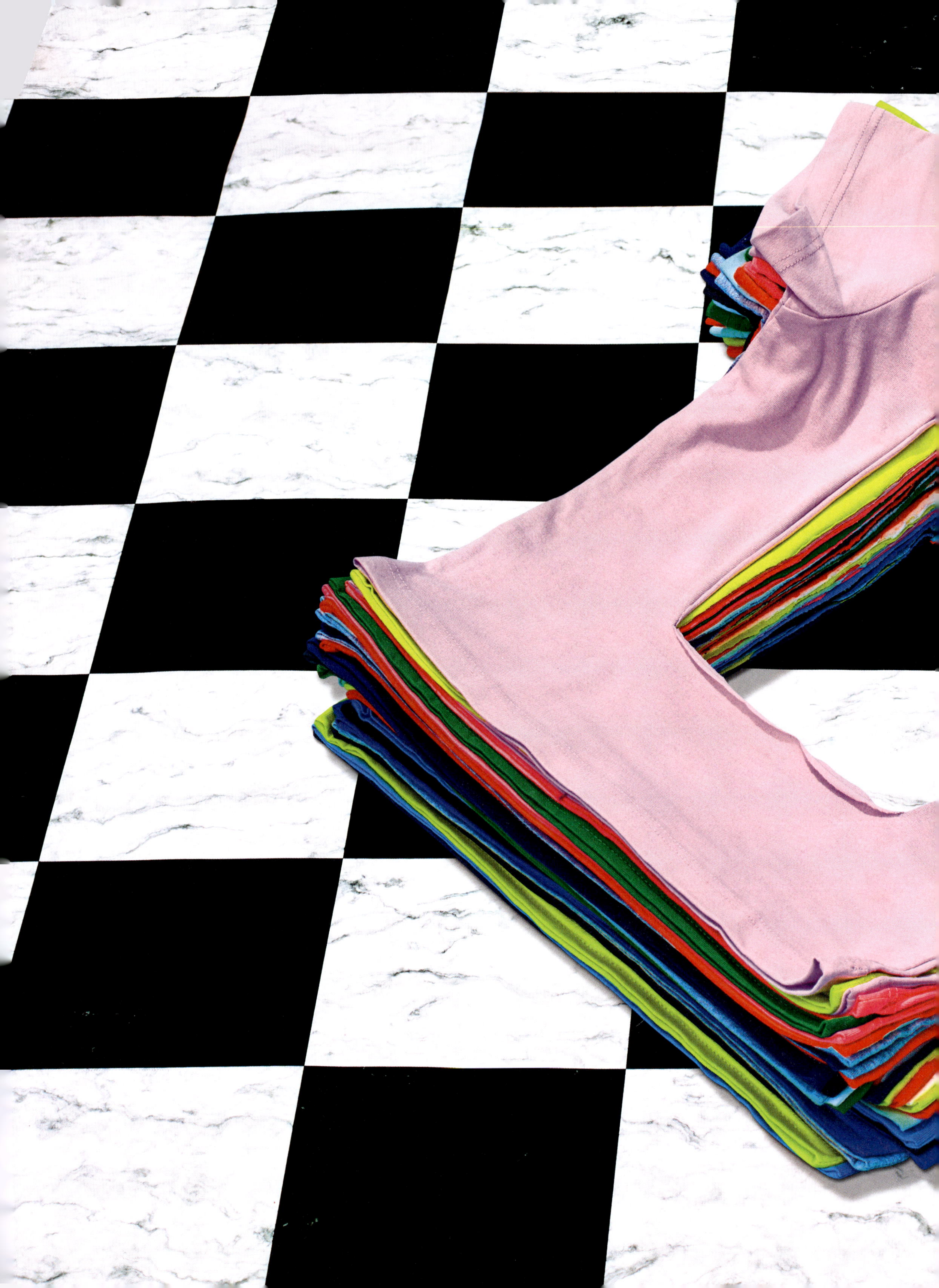

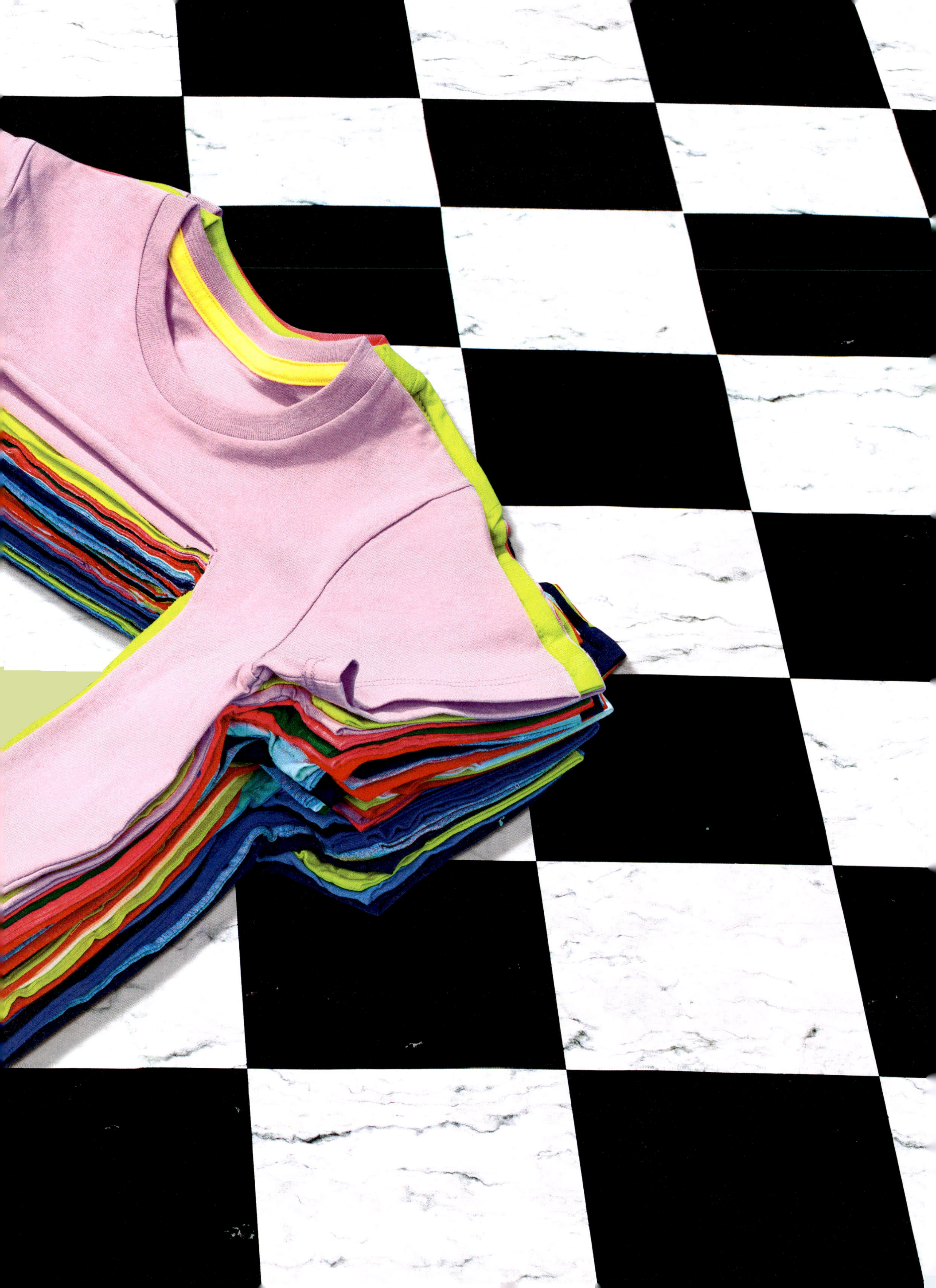

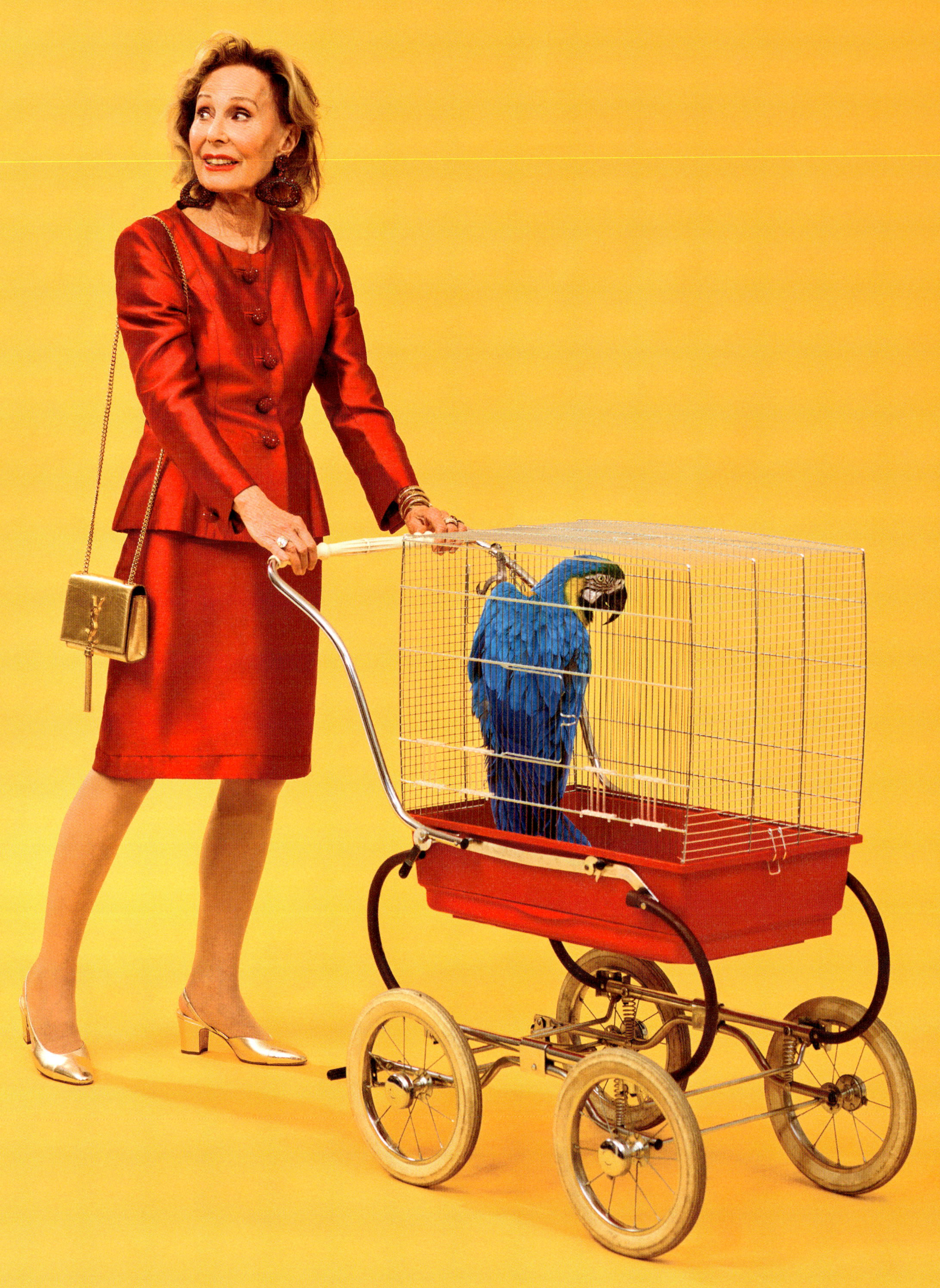

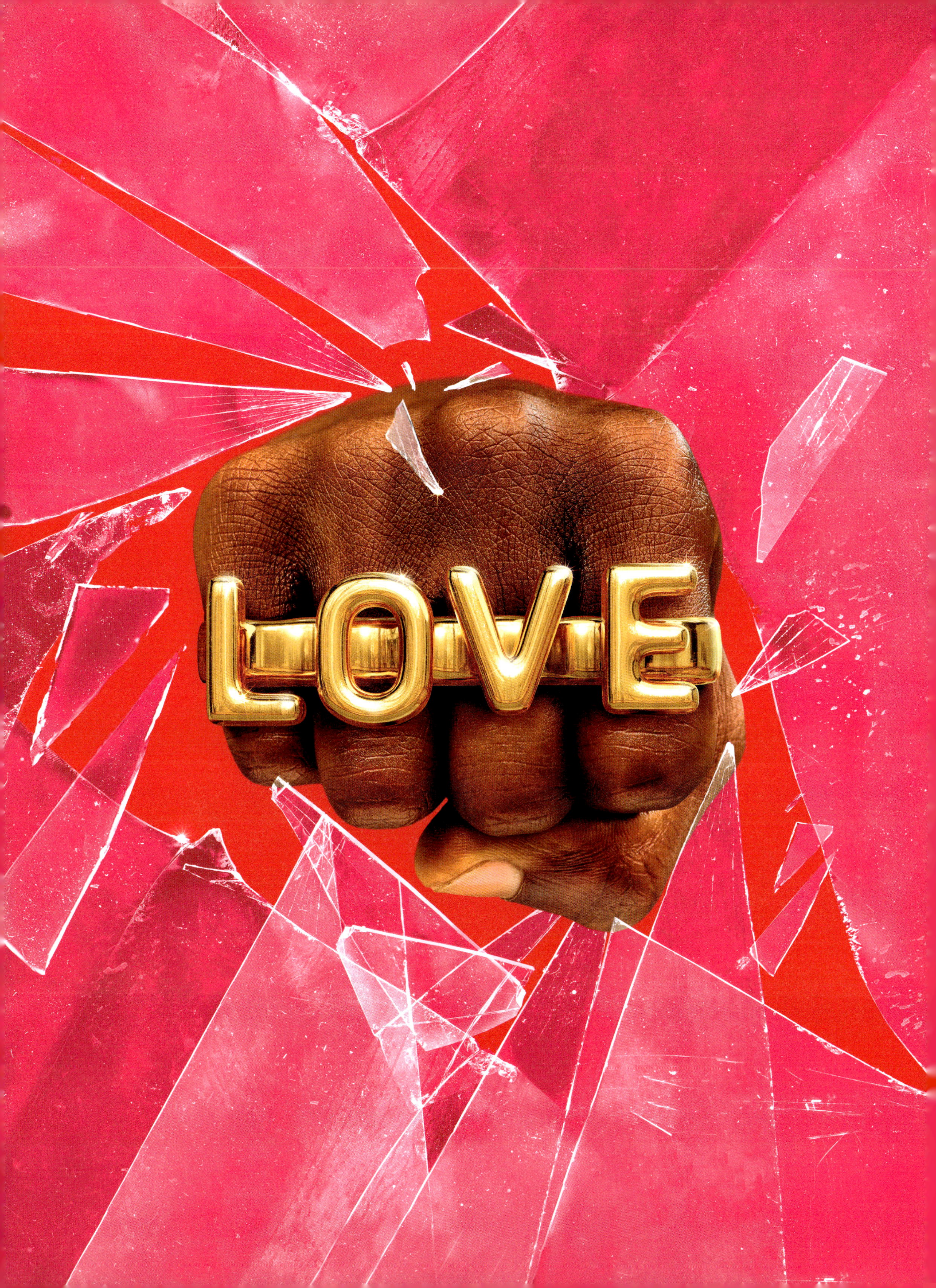

LOVE

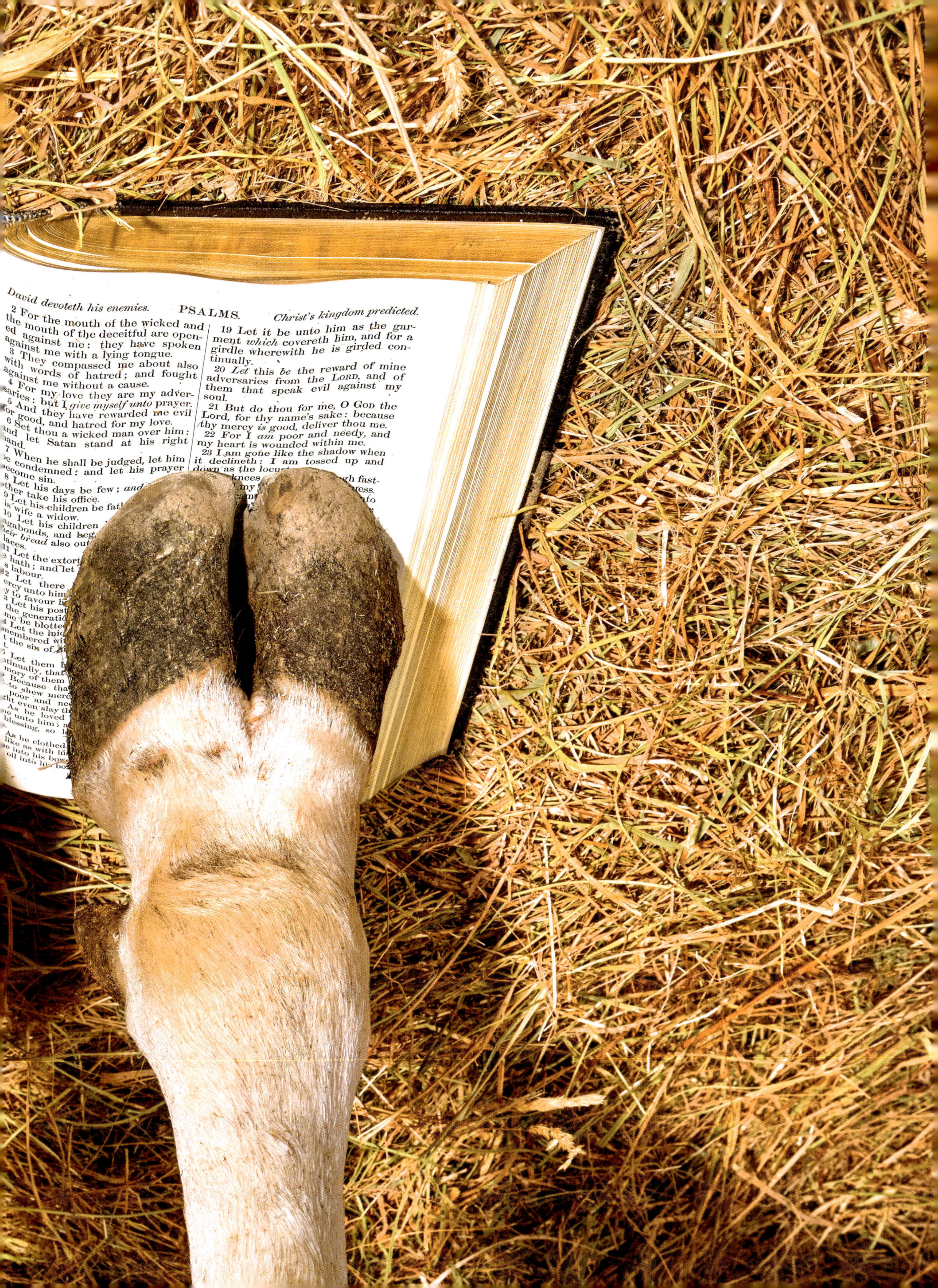

David devoteth his enemies.   PSALMS.   Christ's kingdom predicted.

2 For the mouth of the wicked and the mouth of the deceitful are opened against me: they have spoken against me with a lying tongue.
3 They compassed me about also with words of hatred; and fought against me without a cause.
4 For my love they are my adversaries: but I give myself unto prayer.
5 And they have rewarded me evil for good, and hatred for my love.
6 Set thou a wicked man over him: and let Satan stand at his right hand.
7 When he shall be judged, let him be condemned: and let his prayer become sin.
8 Let his days be few; and let another take his office.
9 Let his children be fatherless, and his wife a widow.

19 Let it be unto him as the garment which covereth him, and for a girdle wherewith he is girded continually.
20 Let this be the reward of mine adversaries from the LORD, and of them that speak evil against my soul.
21 But do thou for me, O GOD the Lord, for thy name's sake: because thy mercy is good, deliver thou me.
22 For I am poor and needy, and my heart is wounded within me.
23 I am gone like the shadow when it declineth: I am tossed up and down as the locust.

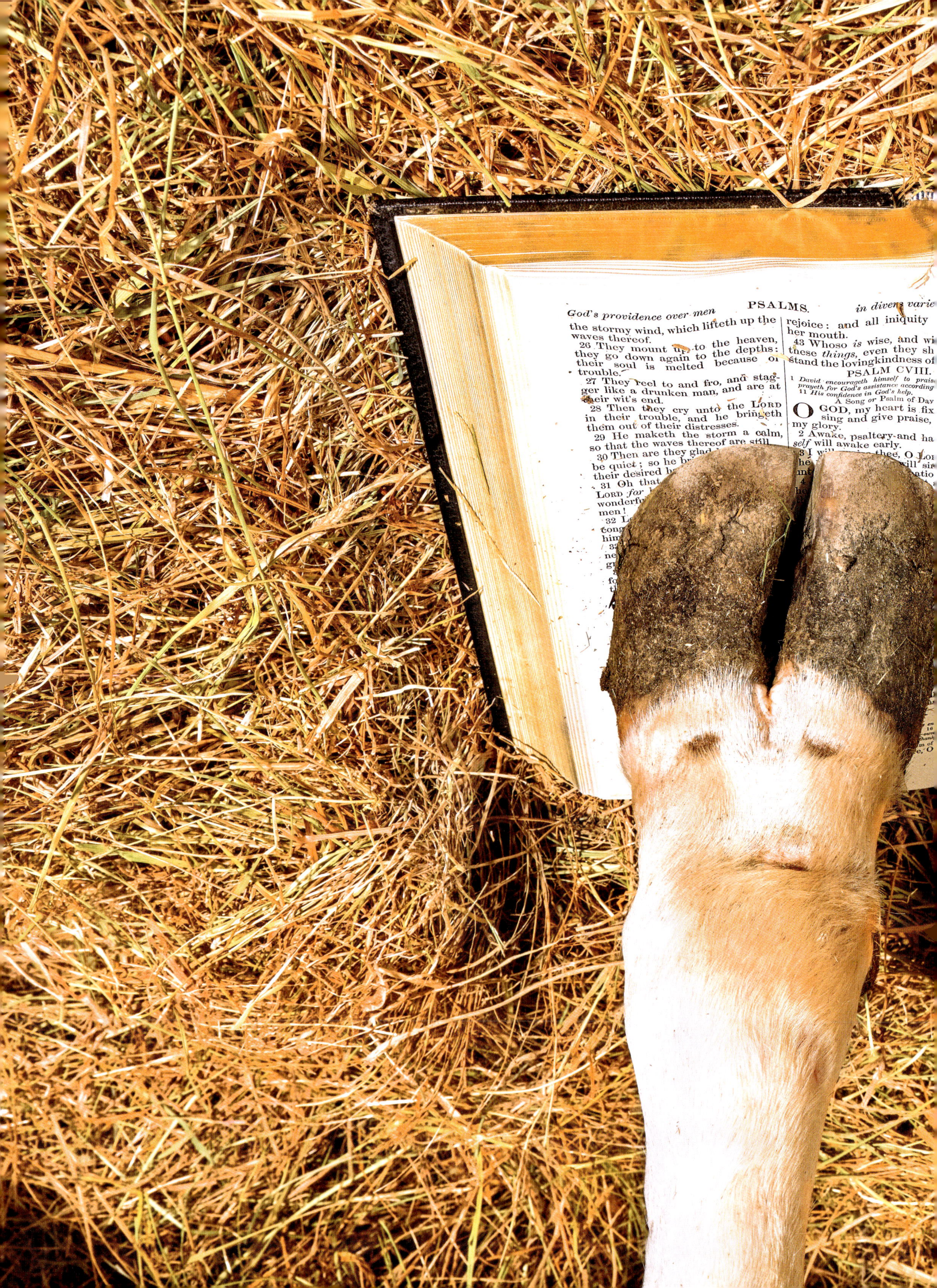

God's providence over men   PSALMS.   in divers varie
the stormy wind, which lifteth up the
waves thereof.
26 They mount up to the heaven, they go down again to the depths: their soul is melted because of trouble.
27 They reel to and fro, and stagger like a drunken man, and are at their wit's end.
28 Then they cry unto the LORD in their trouble, and he bringeth them out of their distresses.
29 He maketh the storm a calm, so that the waves thereof are still.
30 Then are they glad
be quiet; so he br
their desired h
31 Oh that
LORD for
wonderf
men!
32 L
cong
him
ne
rejoice: and all iniquity her mouth.
43 Whoso is wise, and wi these things, even they sh stand the lovingkindness of
PSALM CVIII.
1 David encourageth himself to prais prayeth for God's assistance according 11 His confidence in God's help.
A Song or Psalm of Day
O GOD, my heart is fix sing and give praise, my glory.
2 Awake, psaltery and ha self will awake early.
3 I will thee, O L he will si
4
he

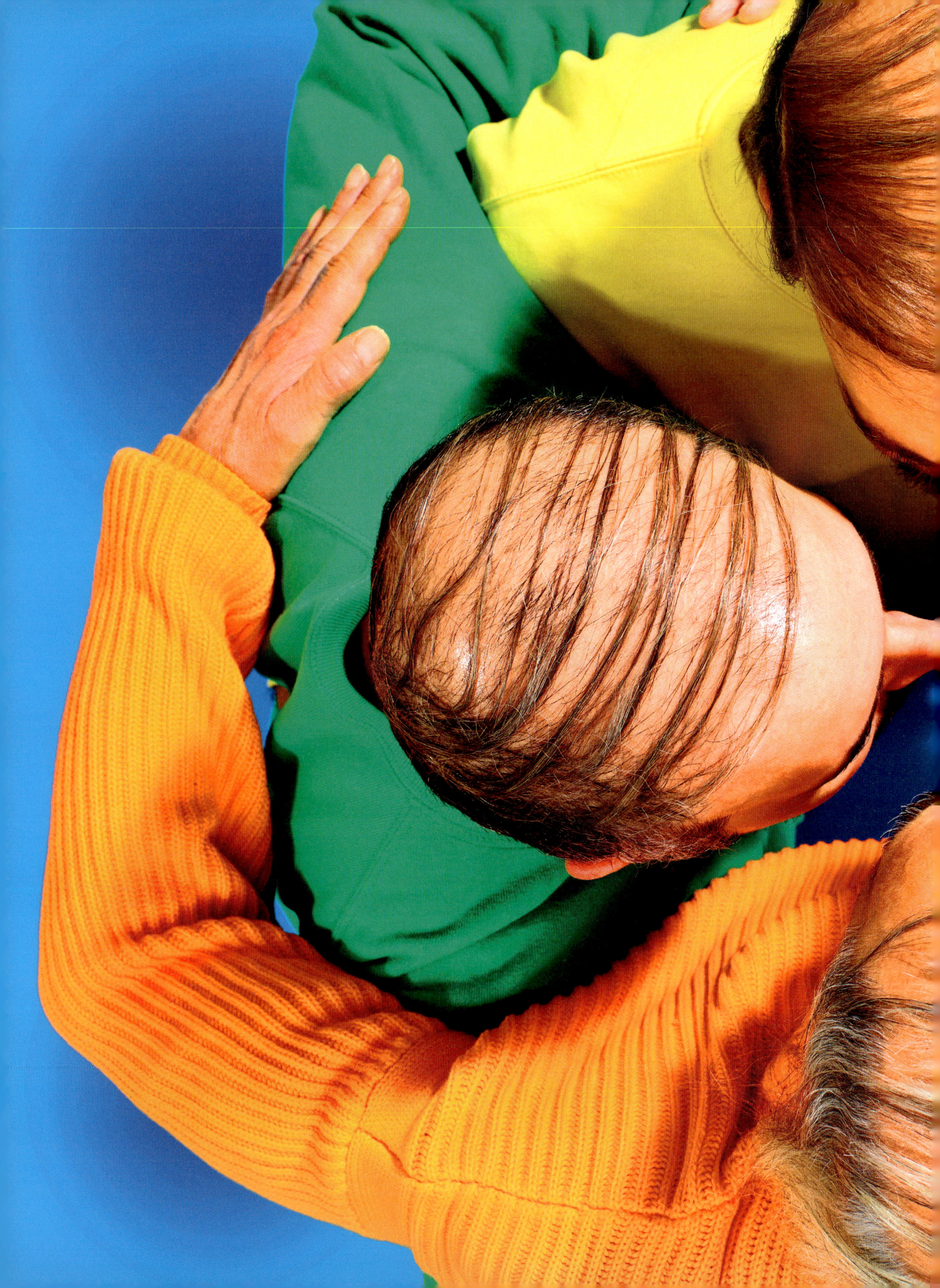

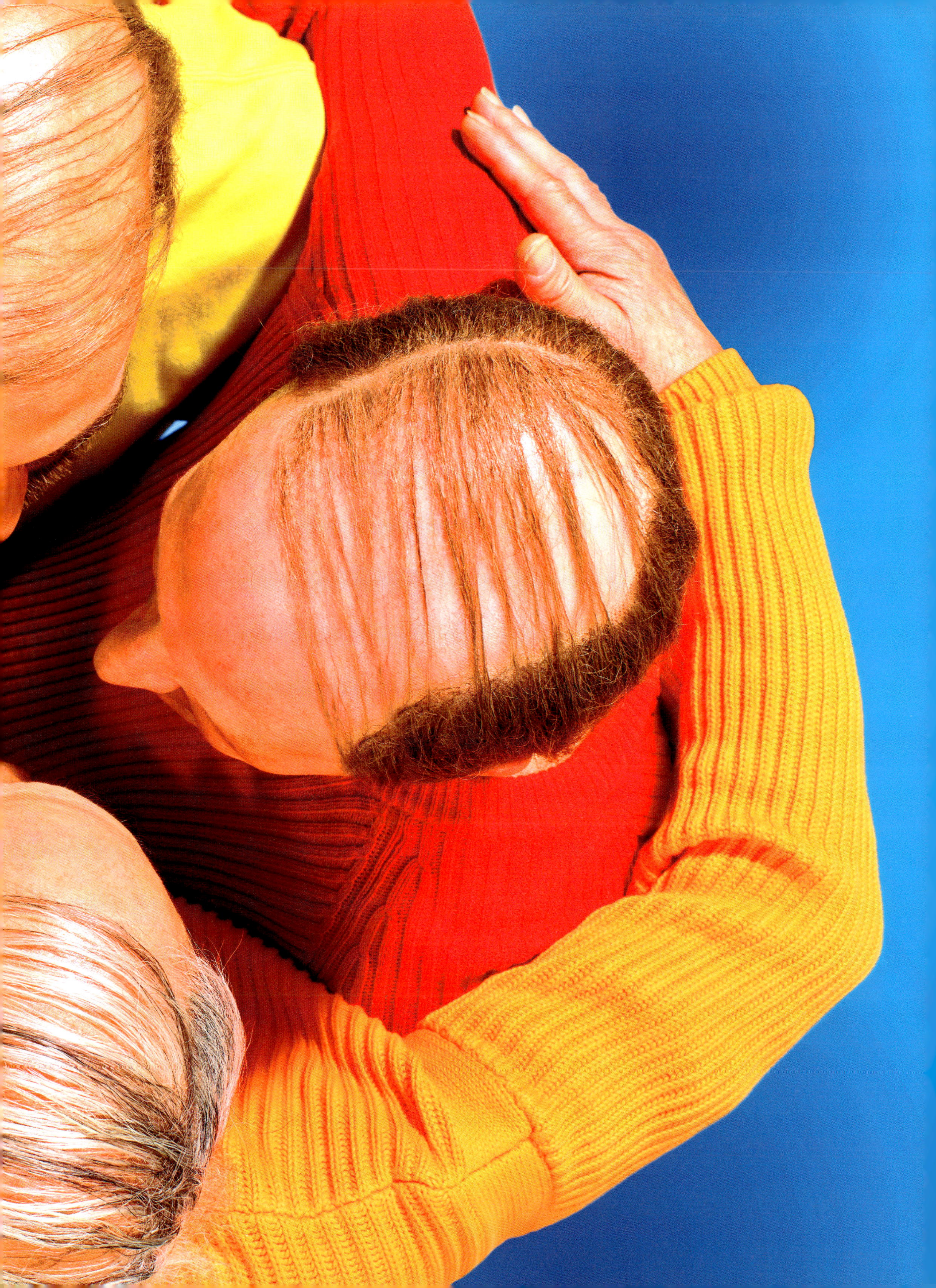

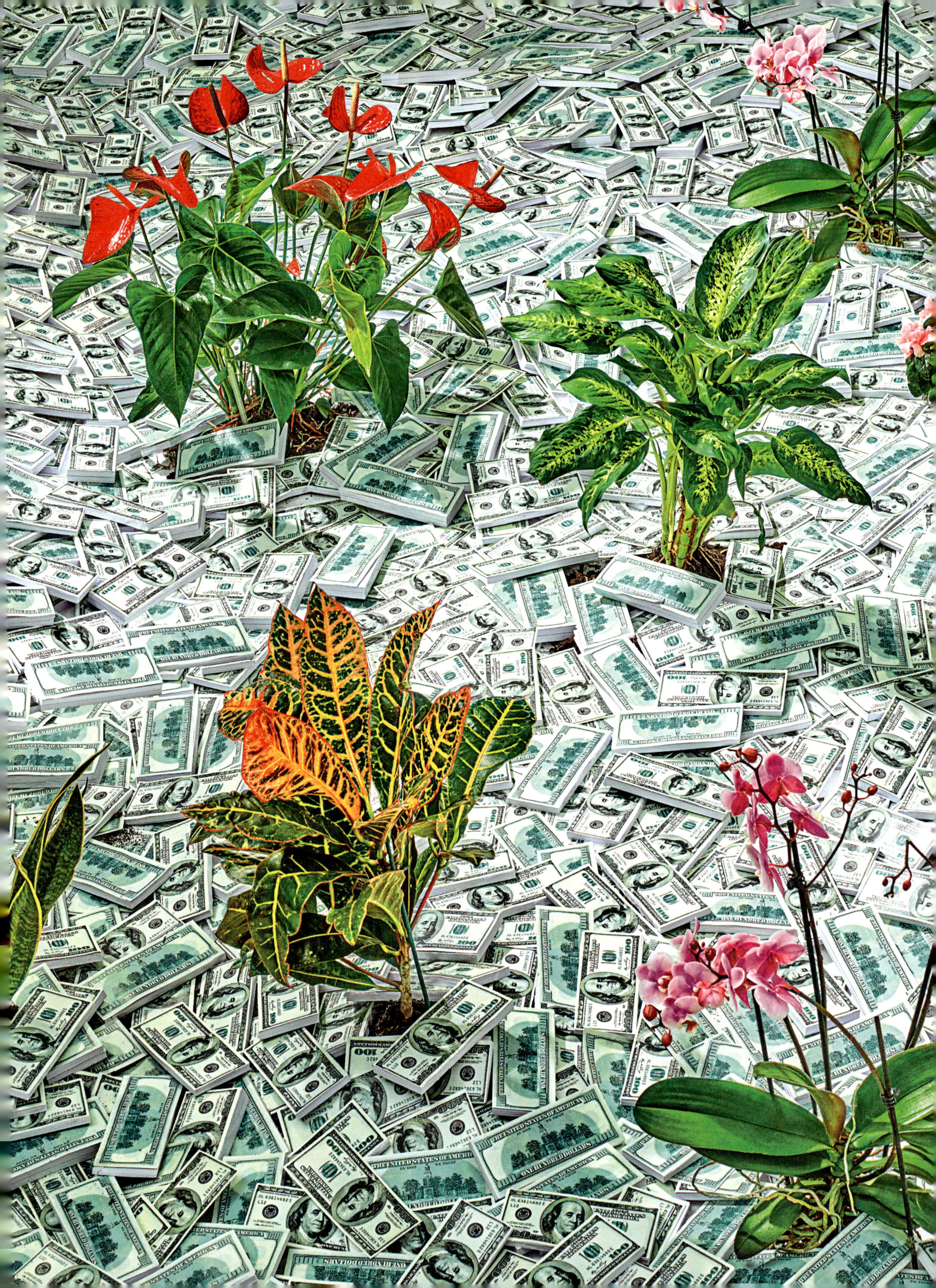

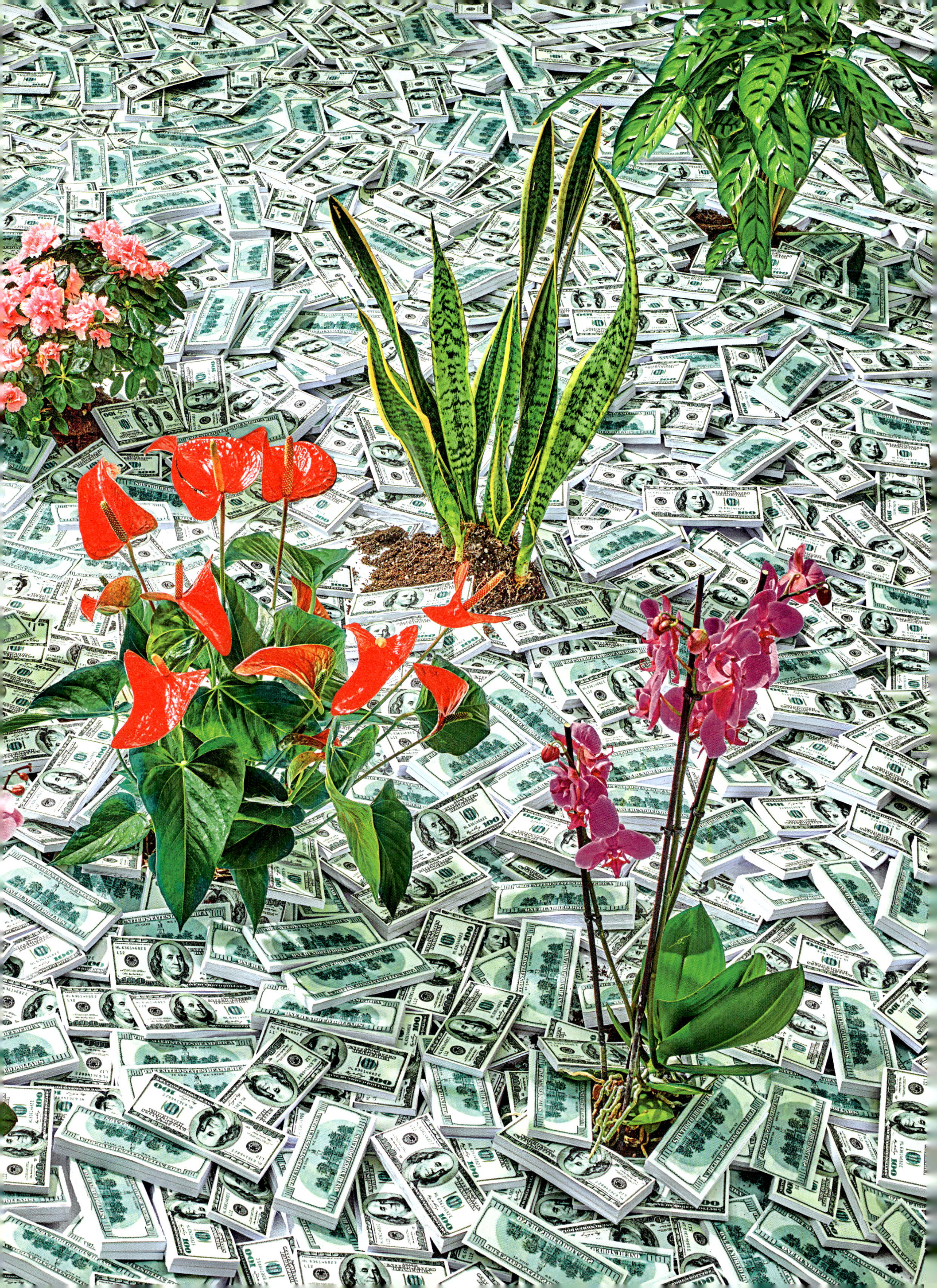

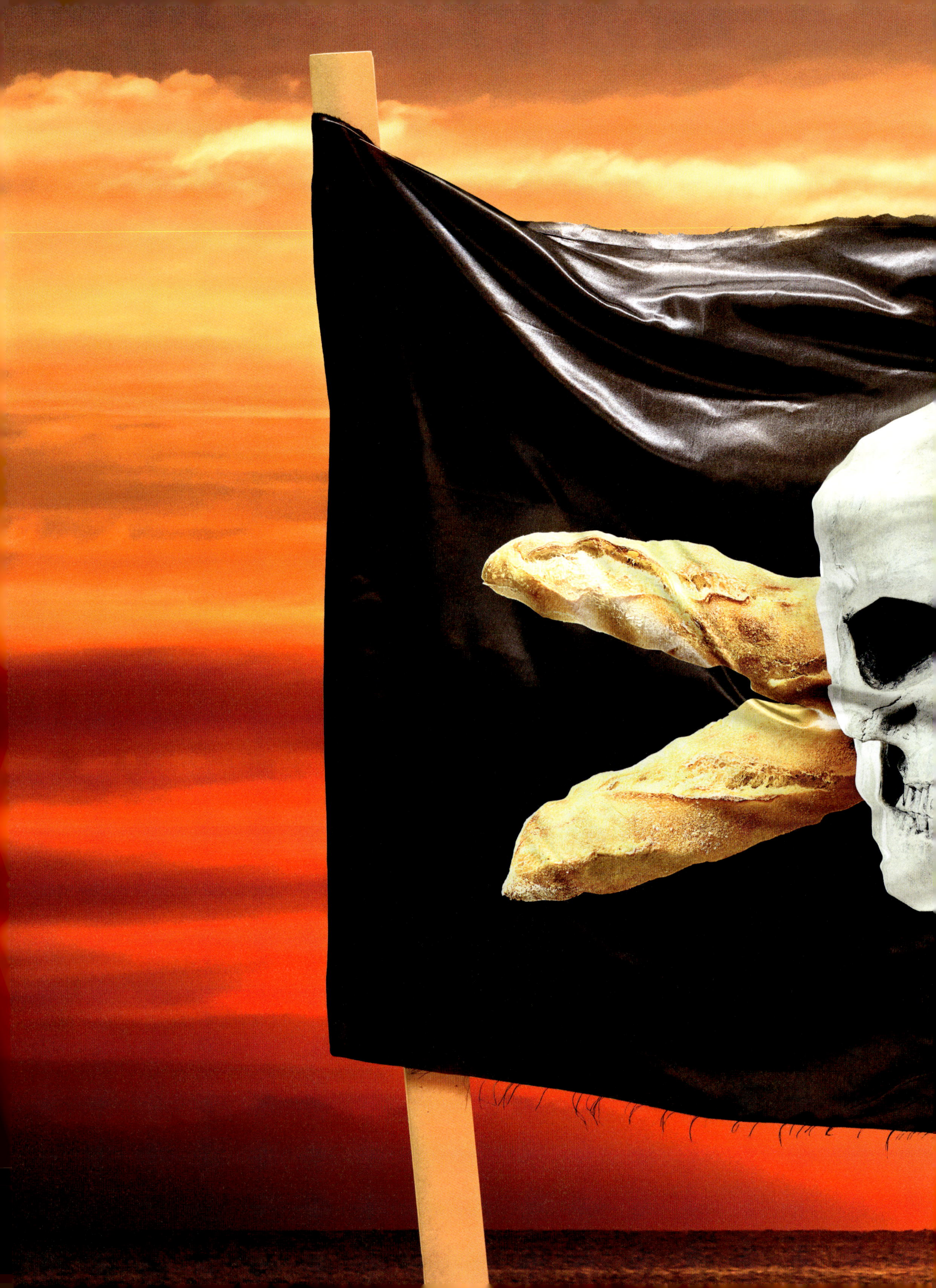

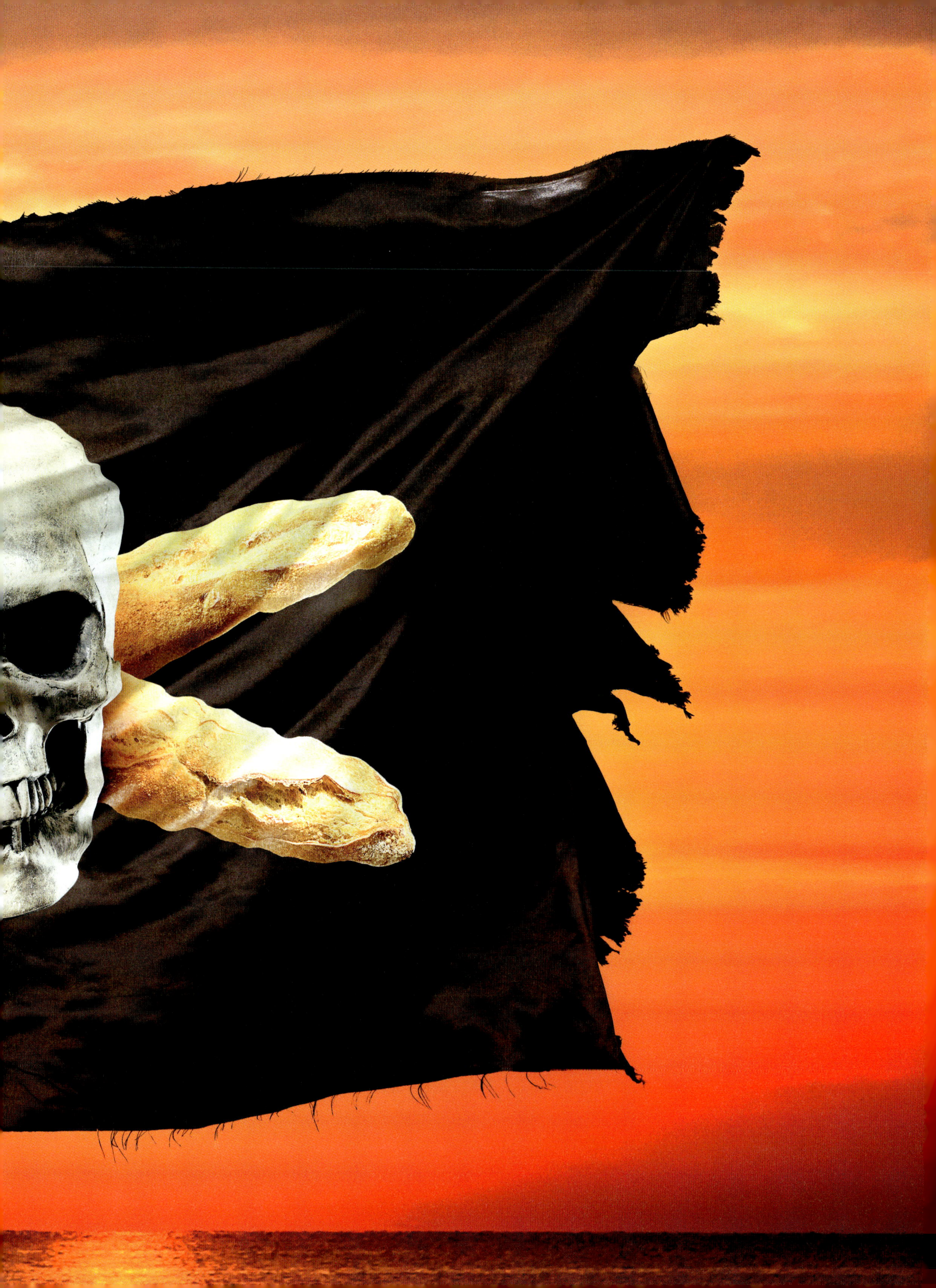

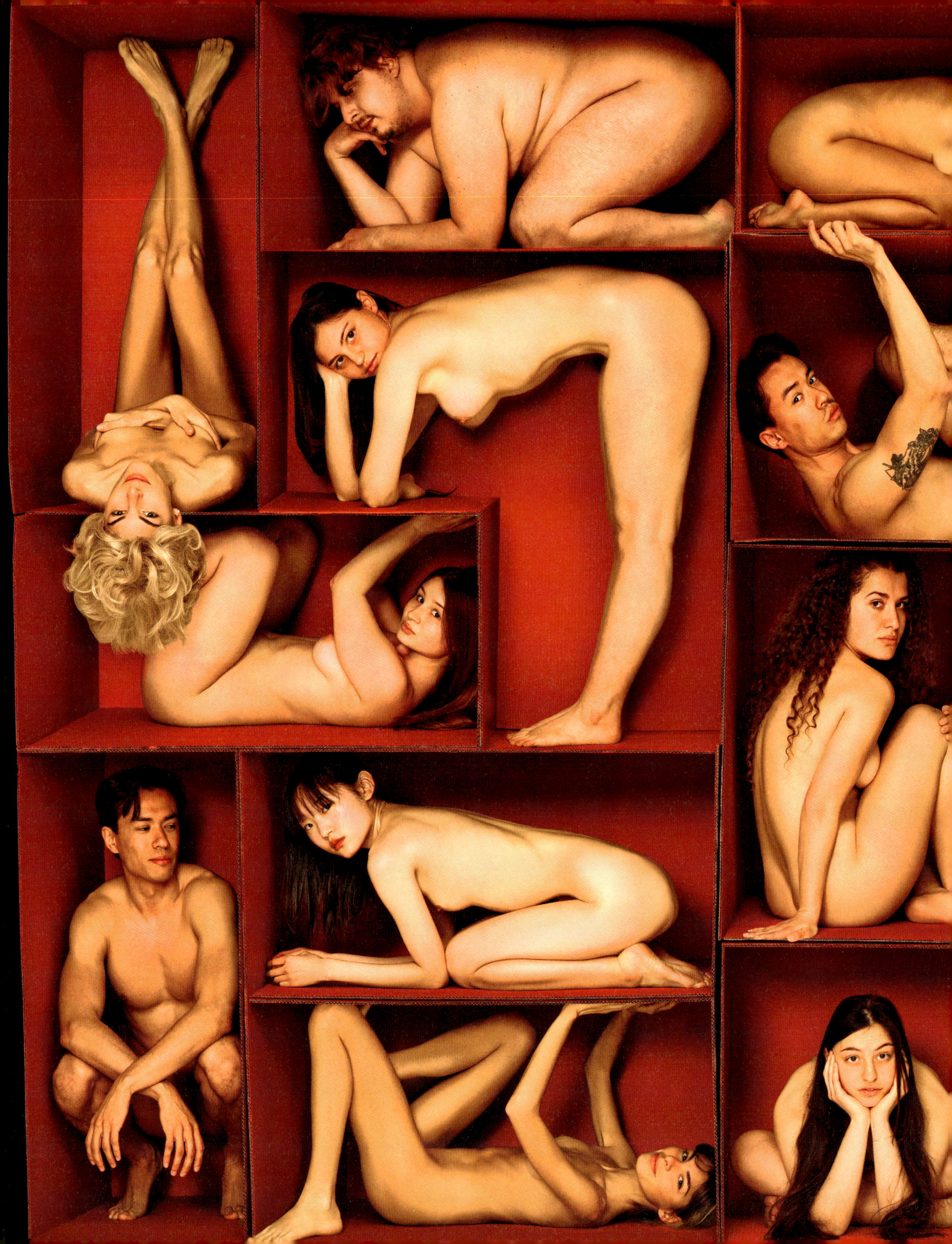

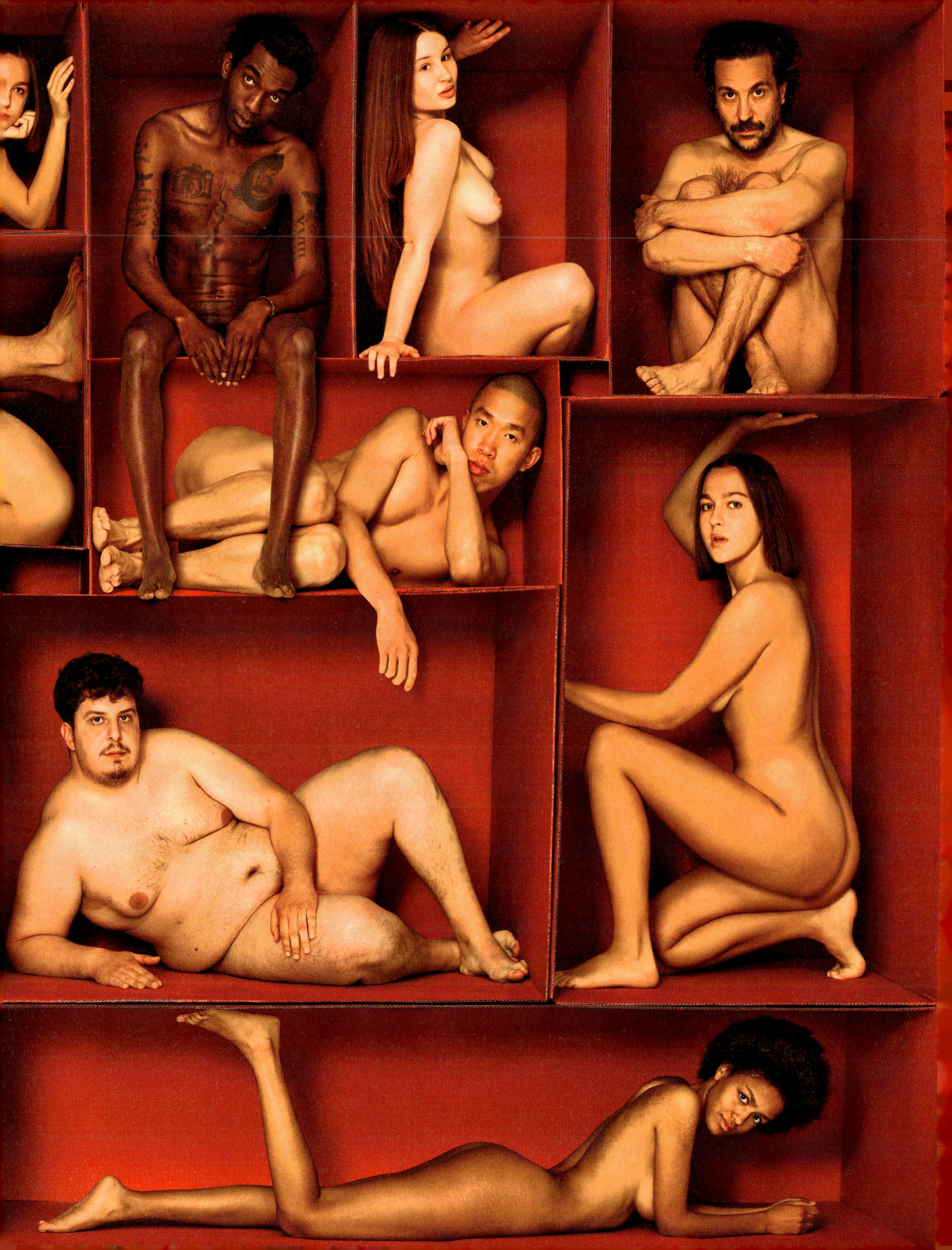

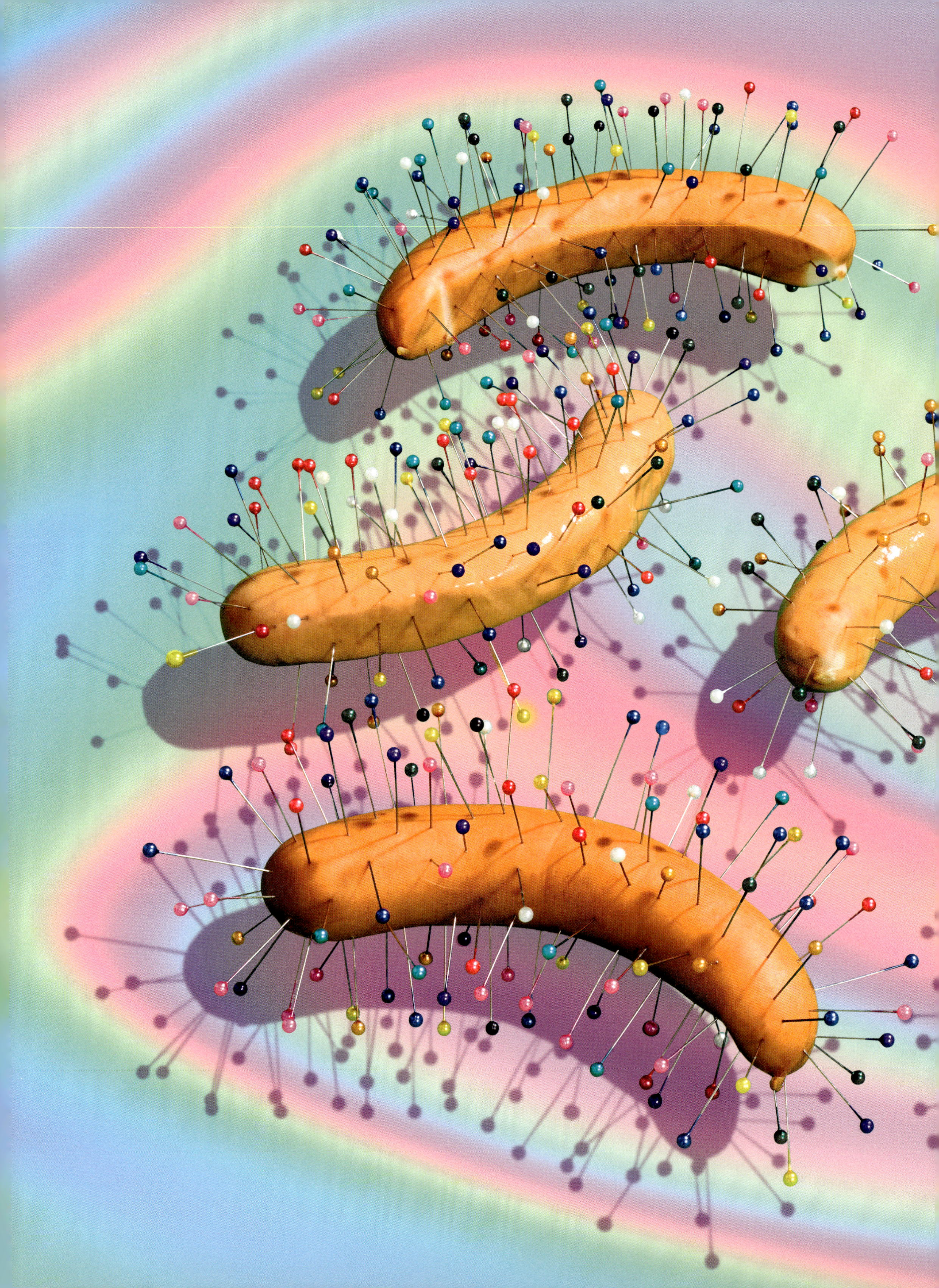

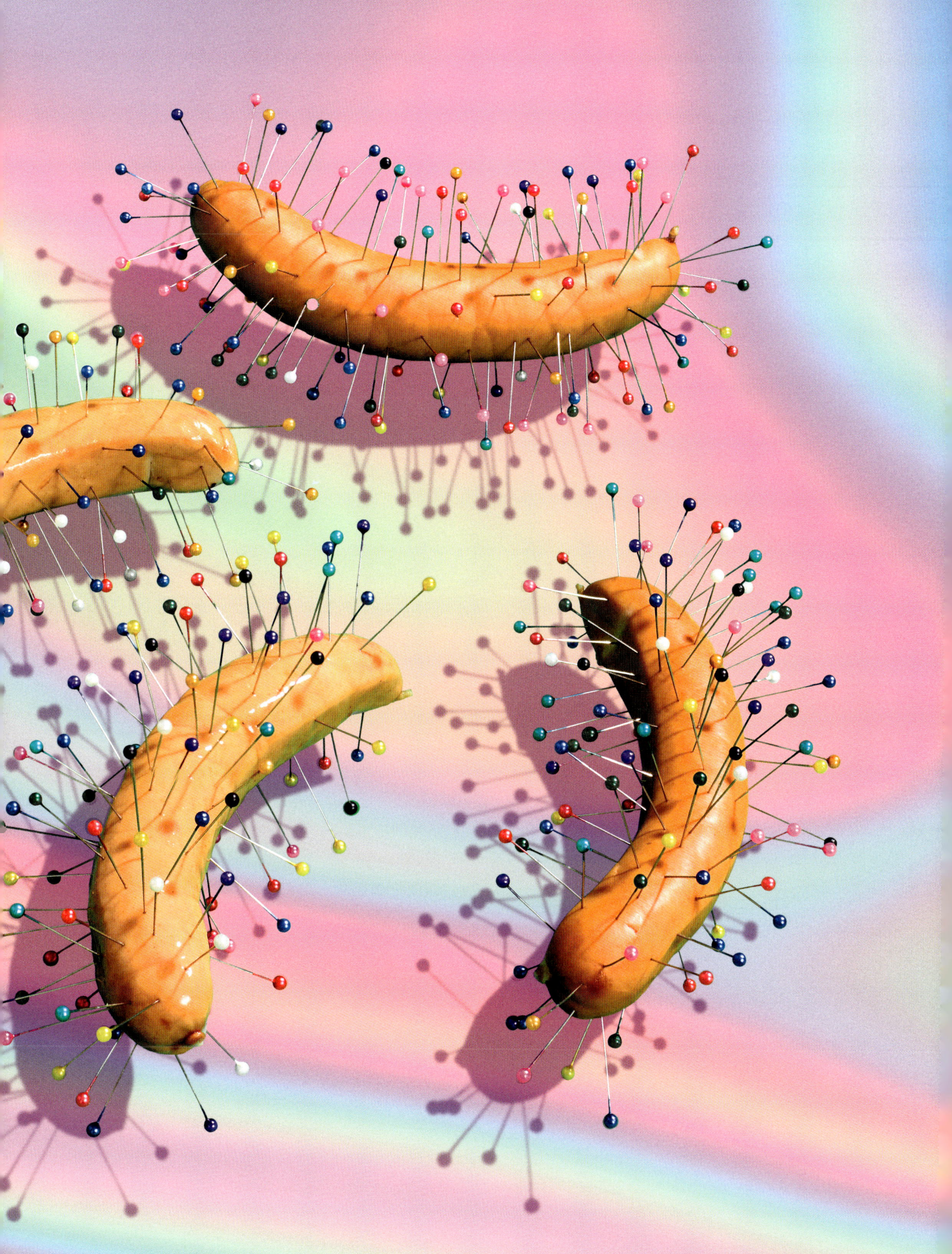

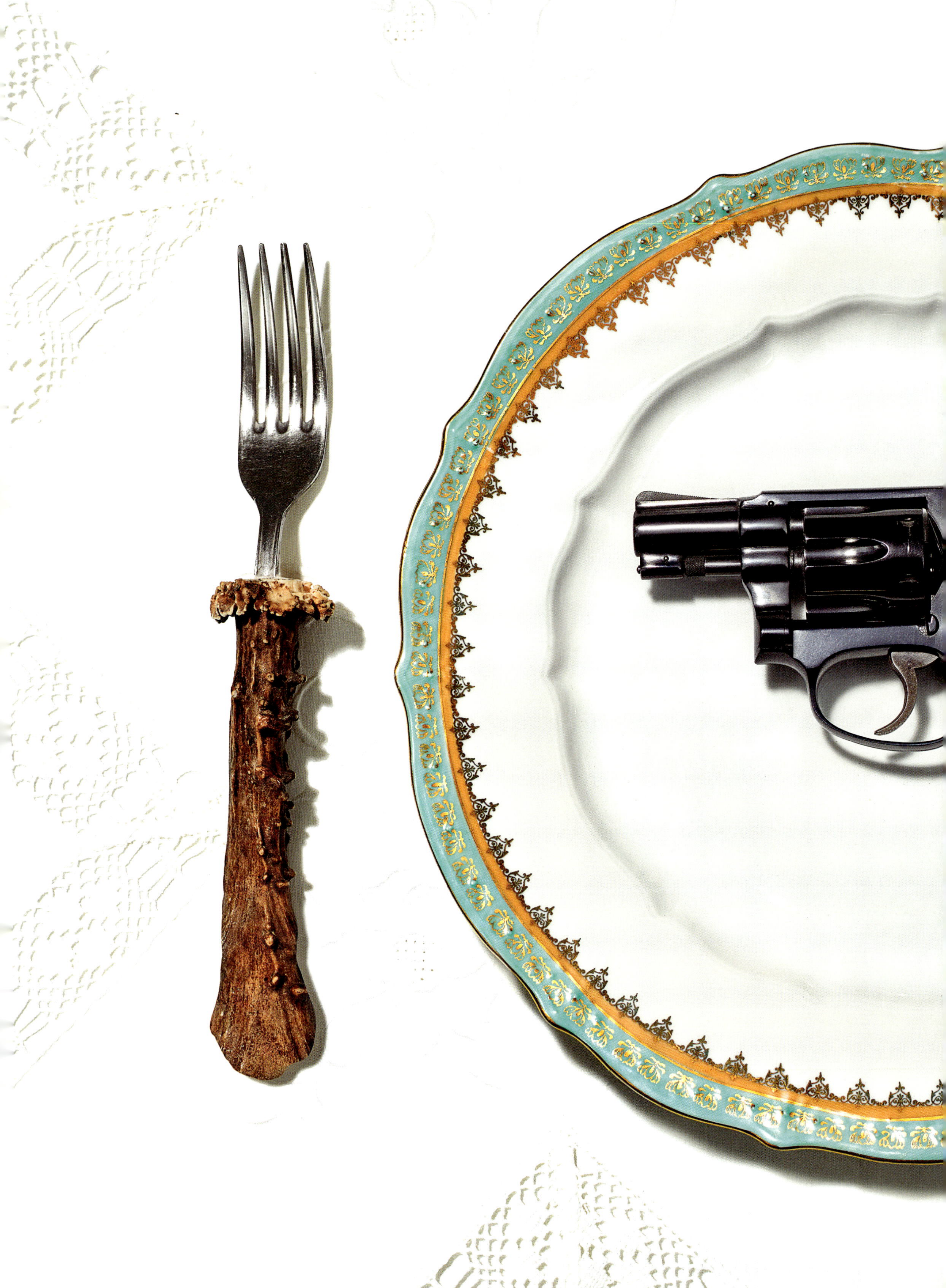

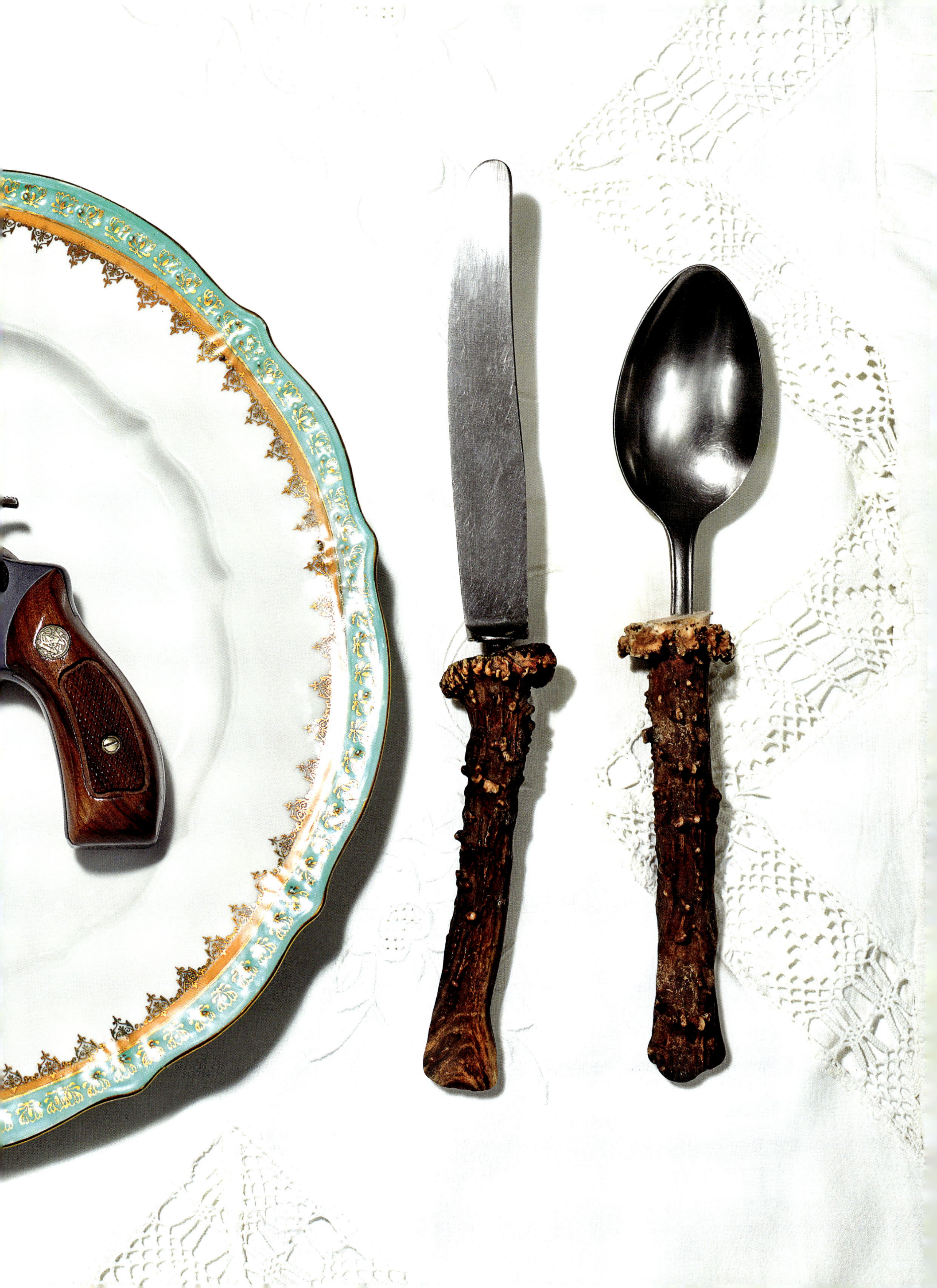

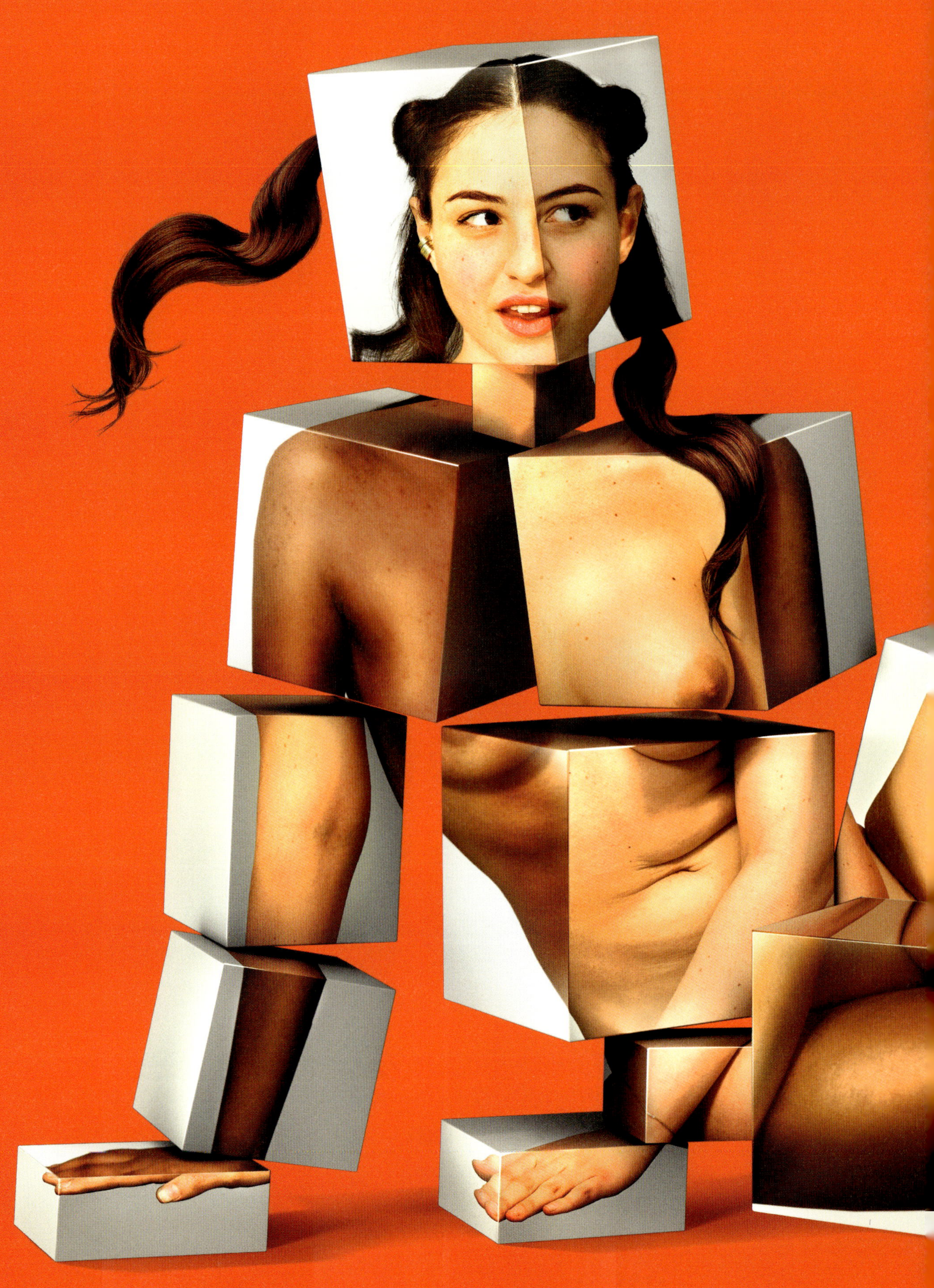

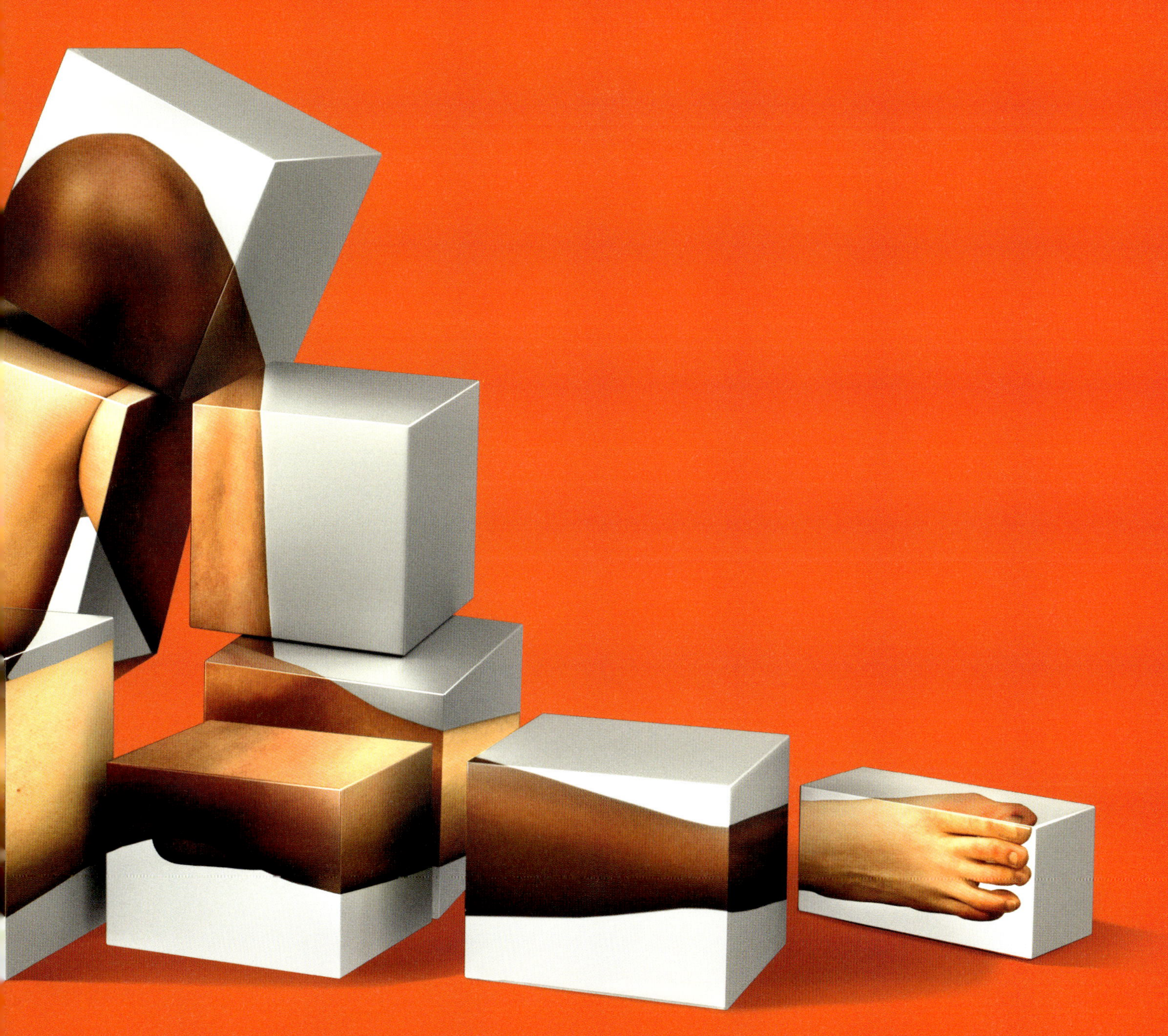

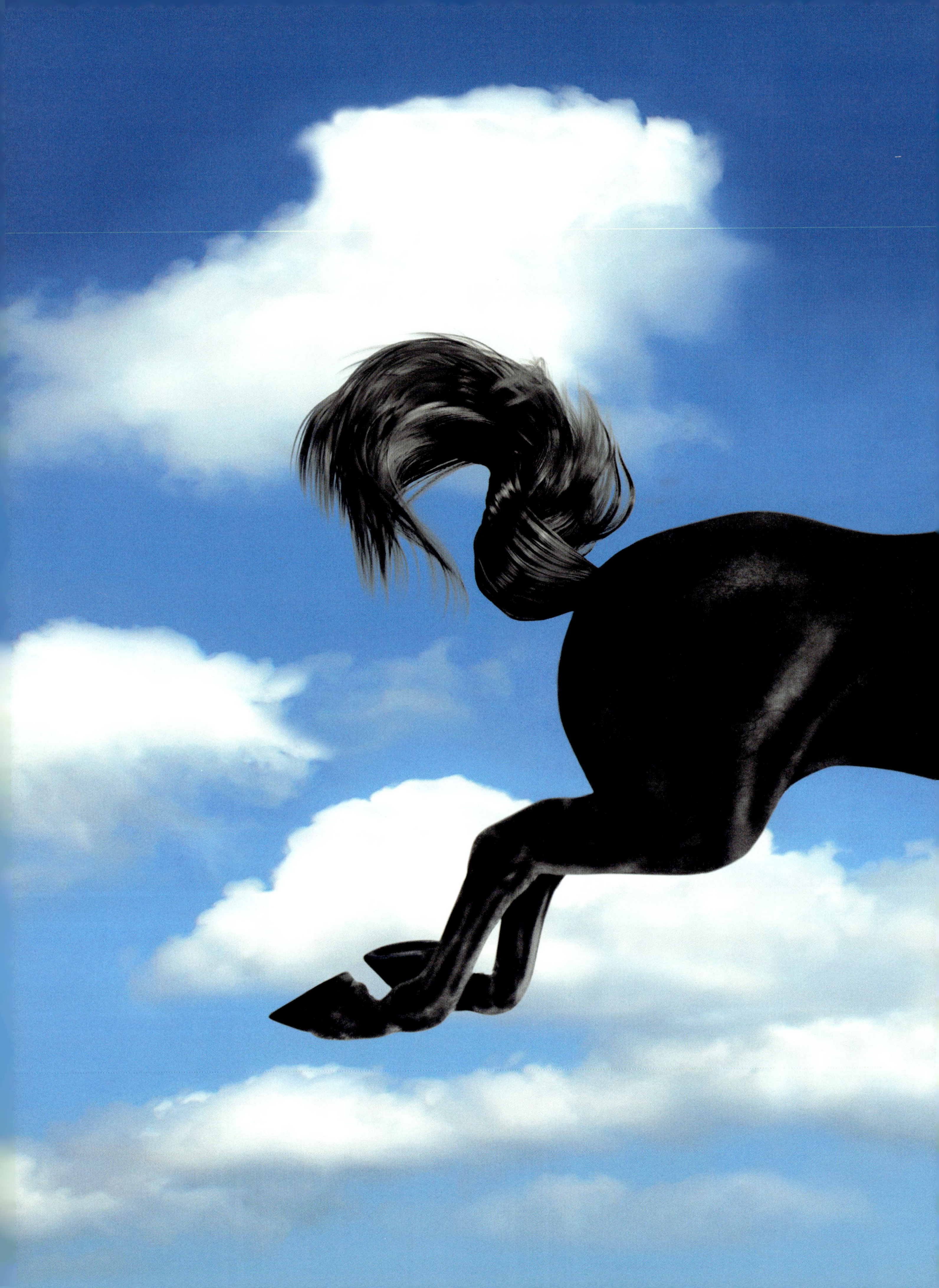

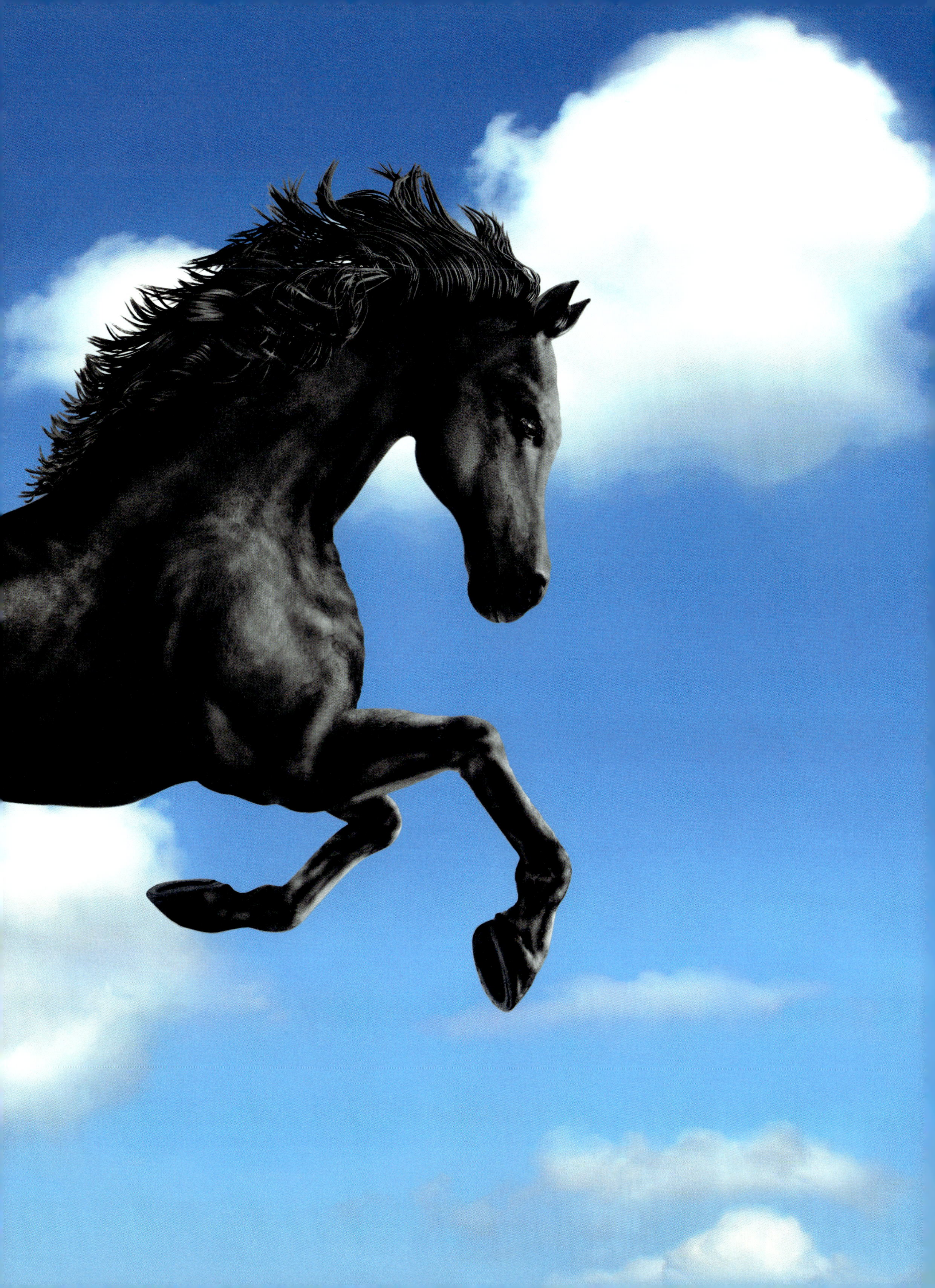

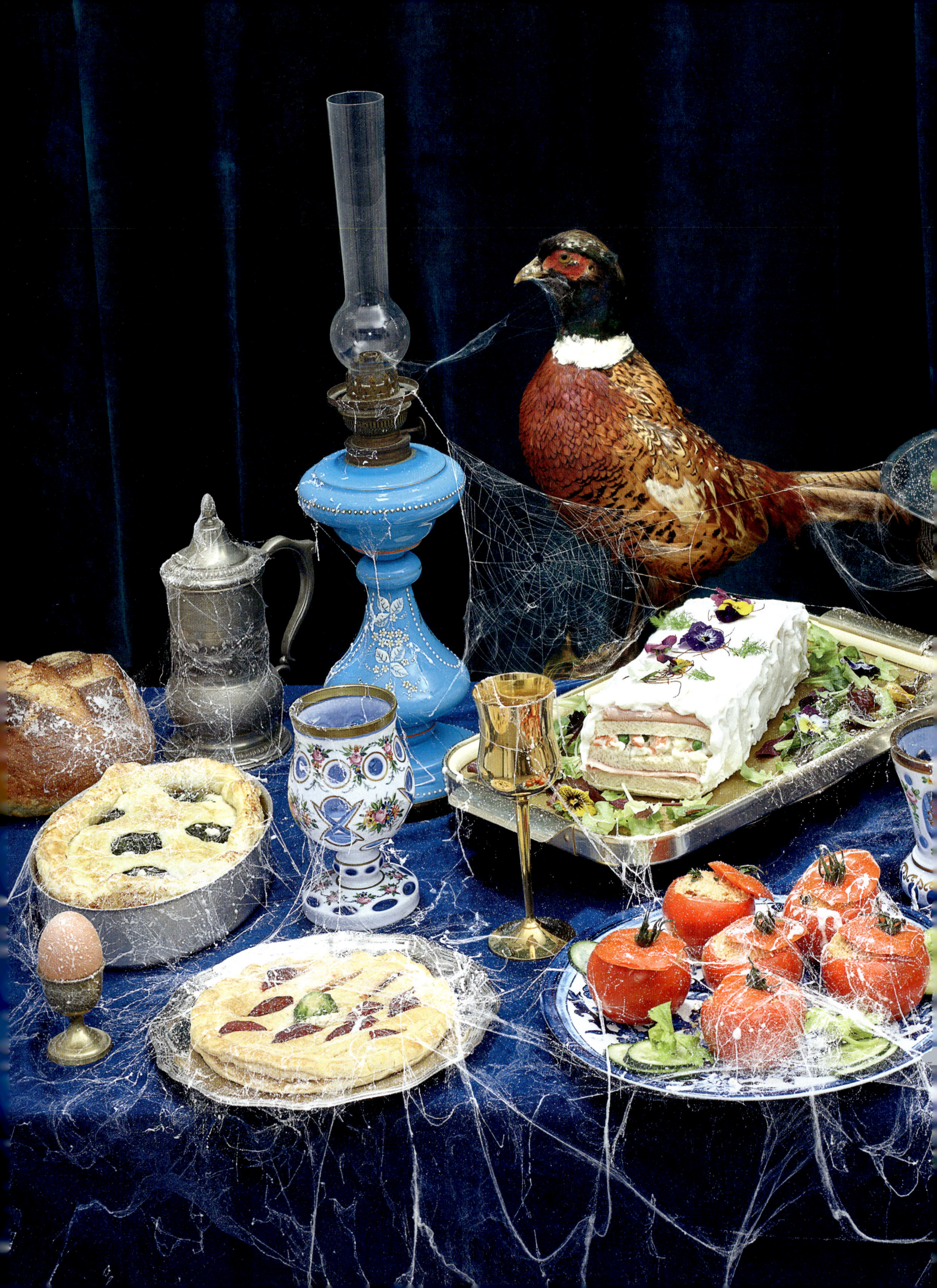

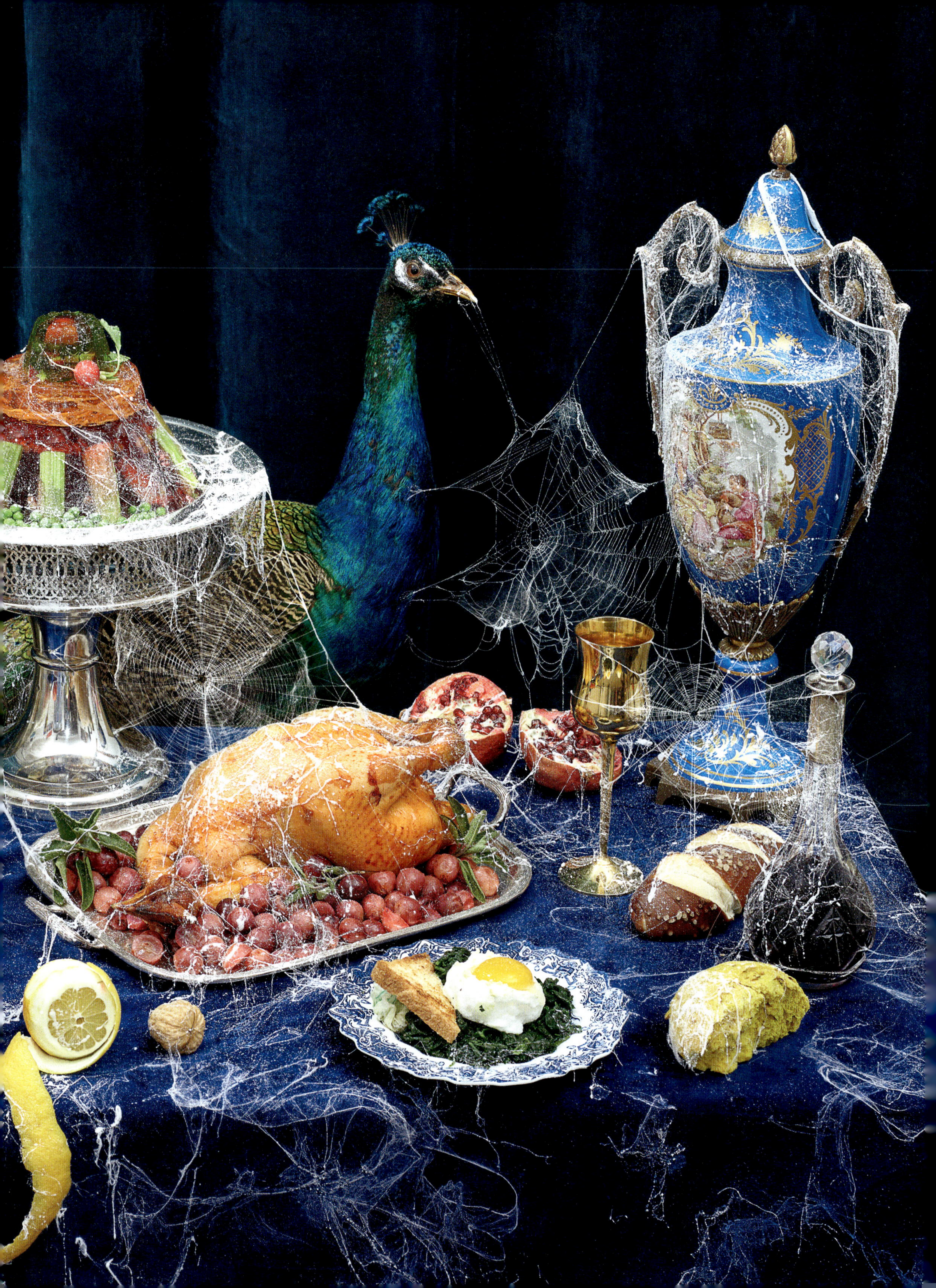

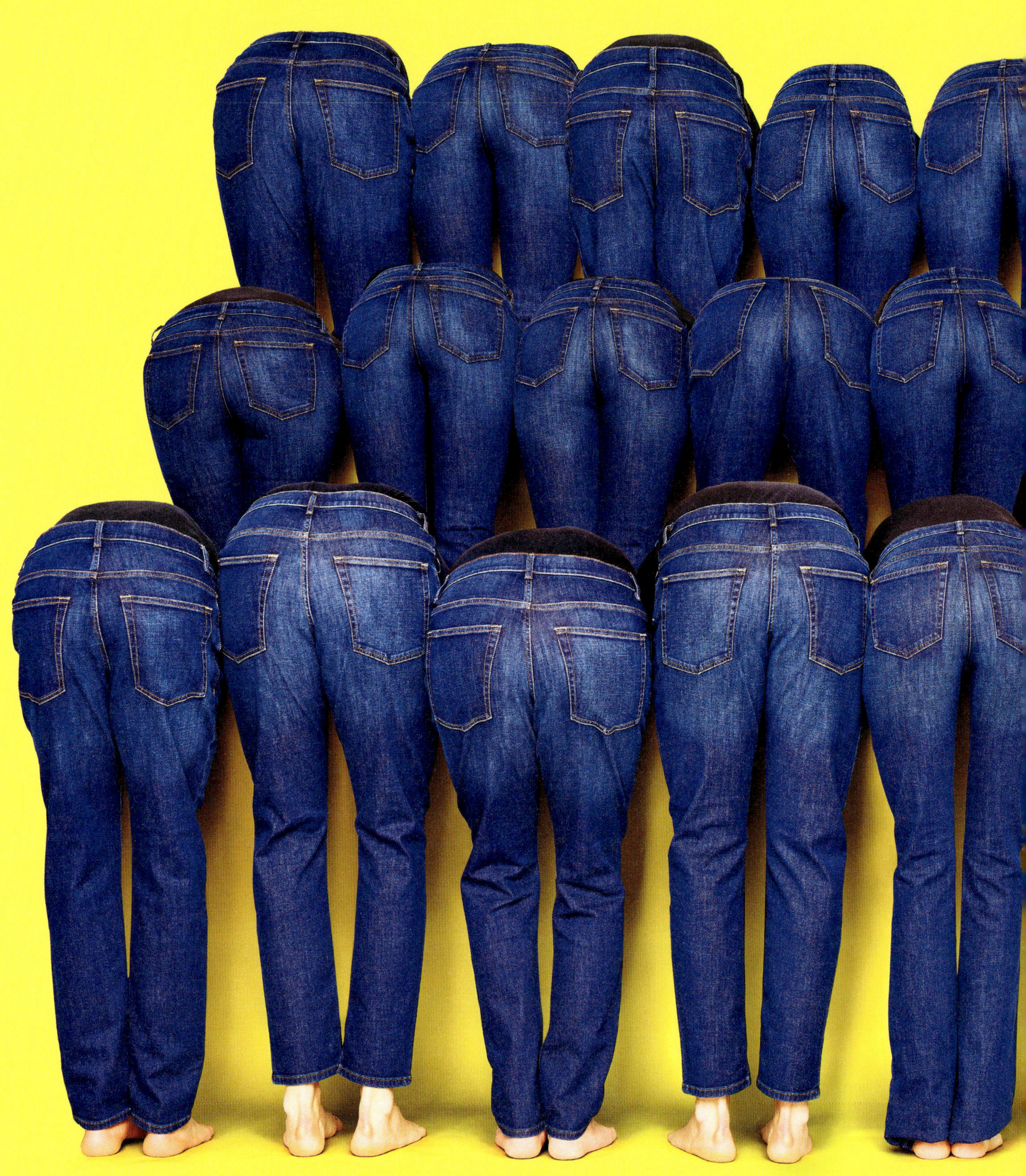

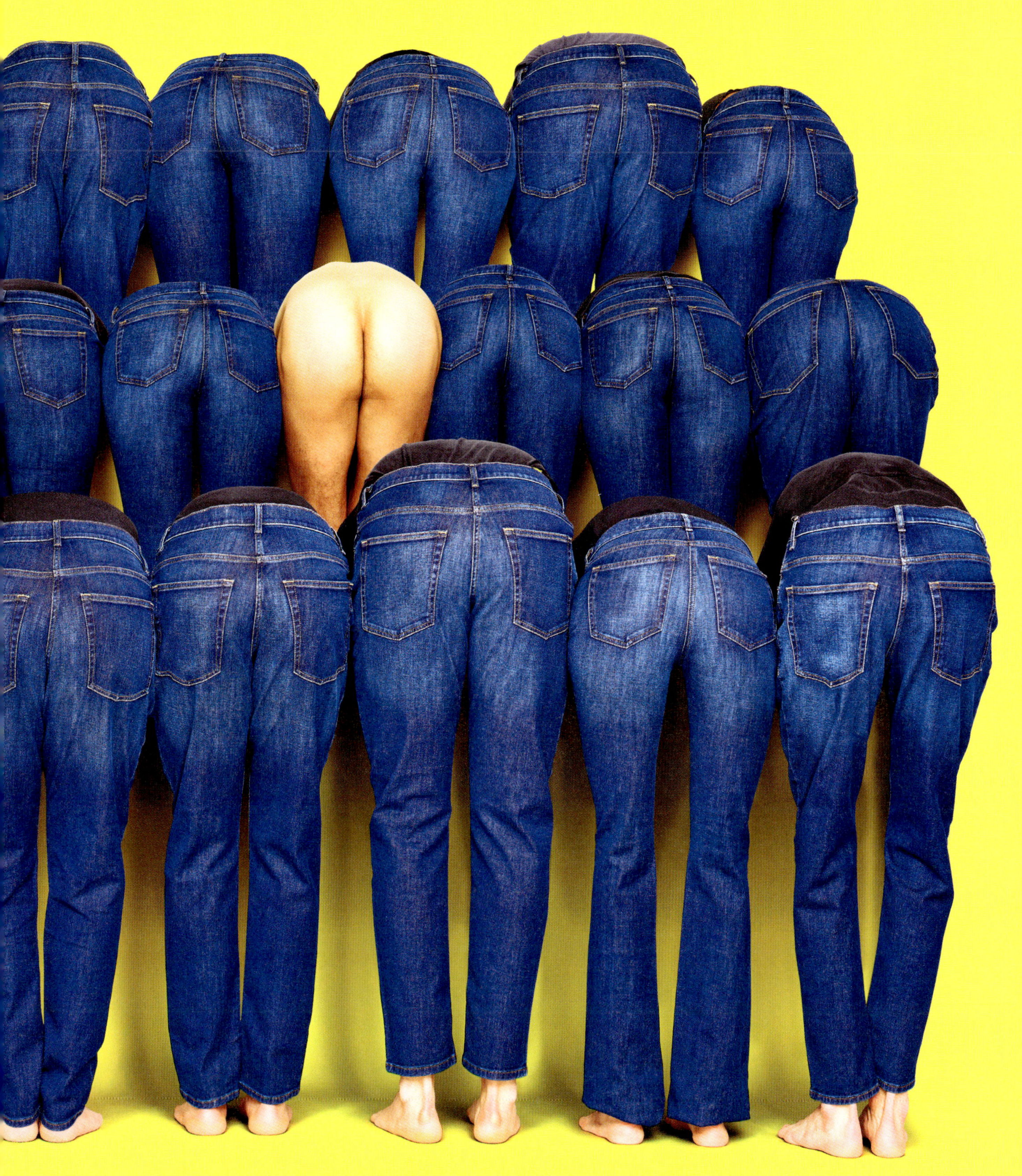

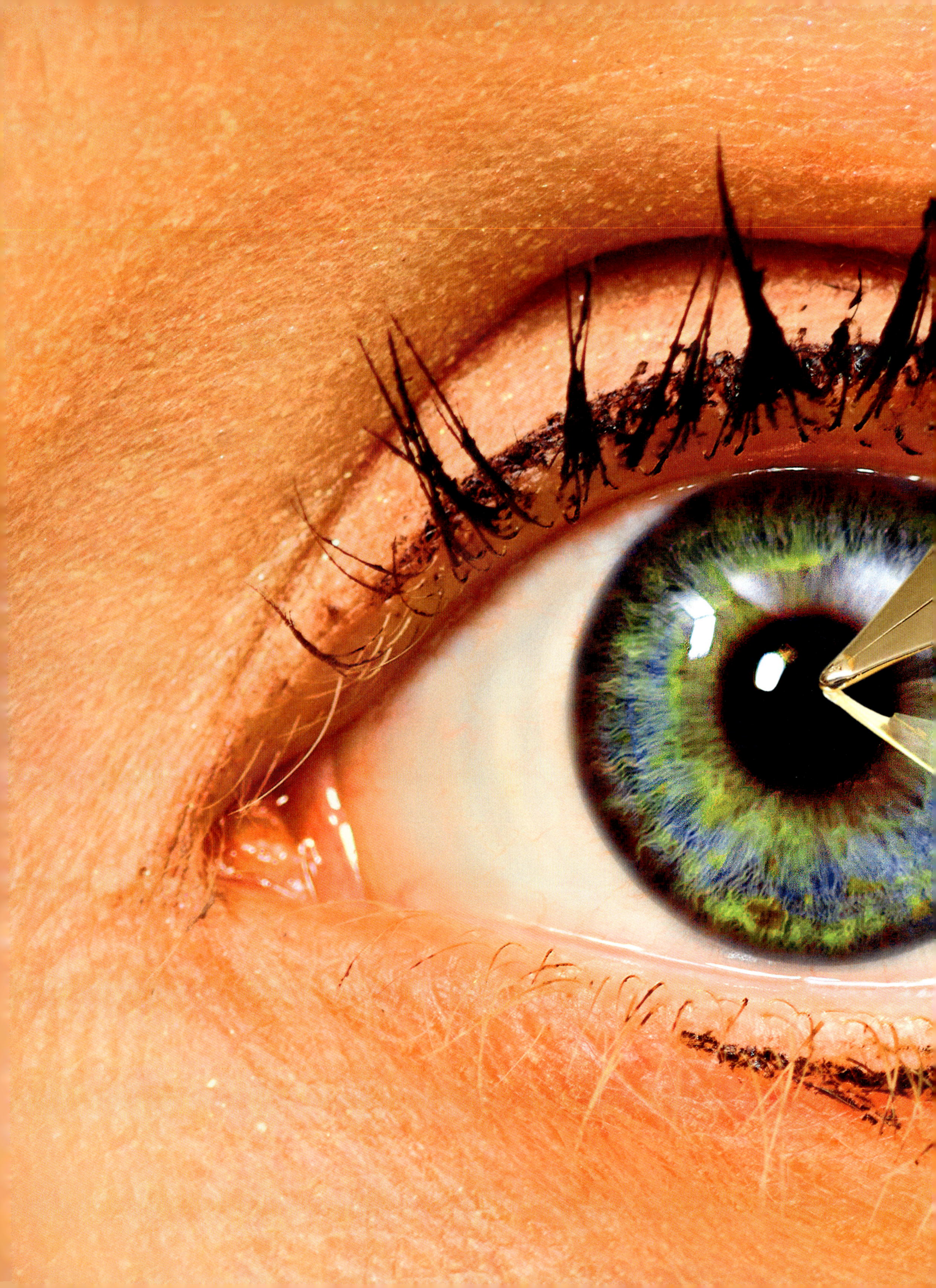

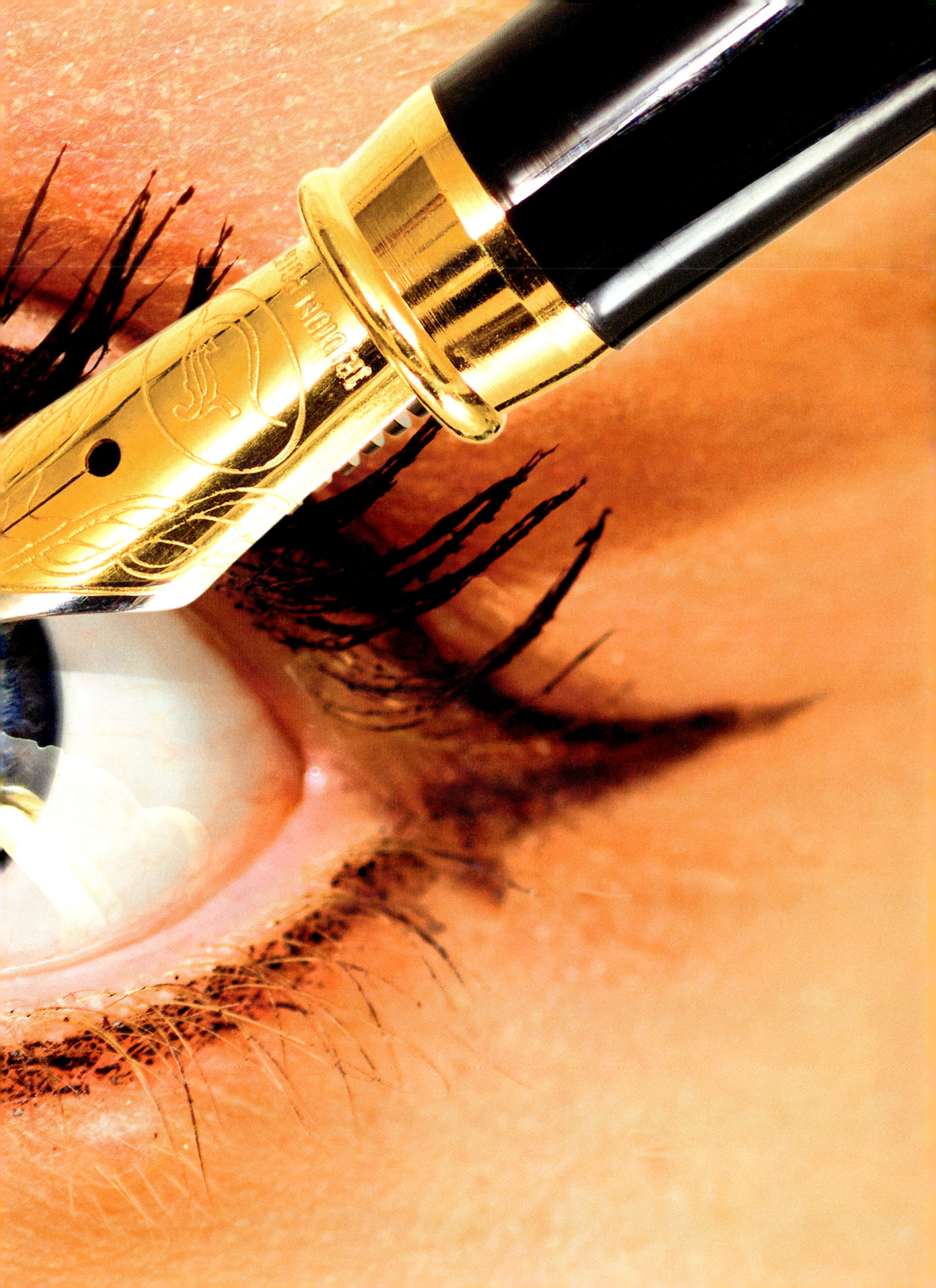

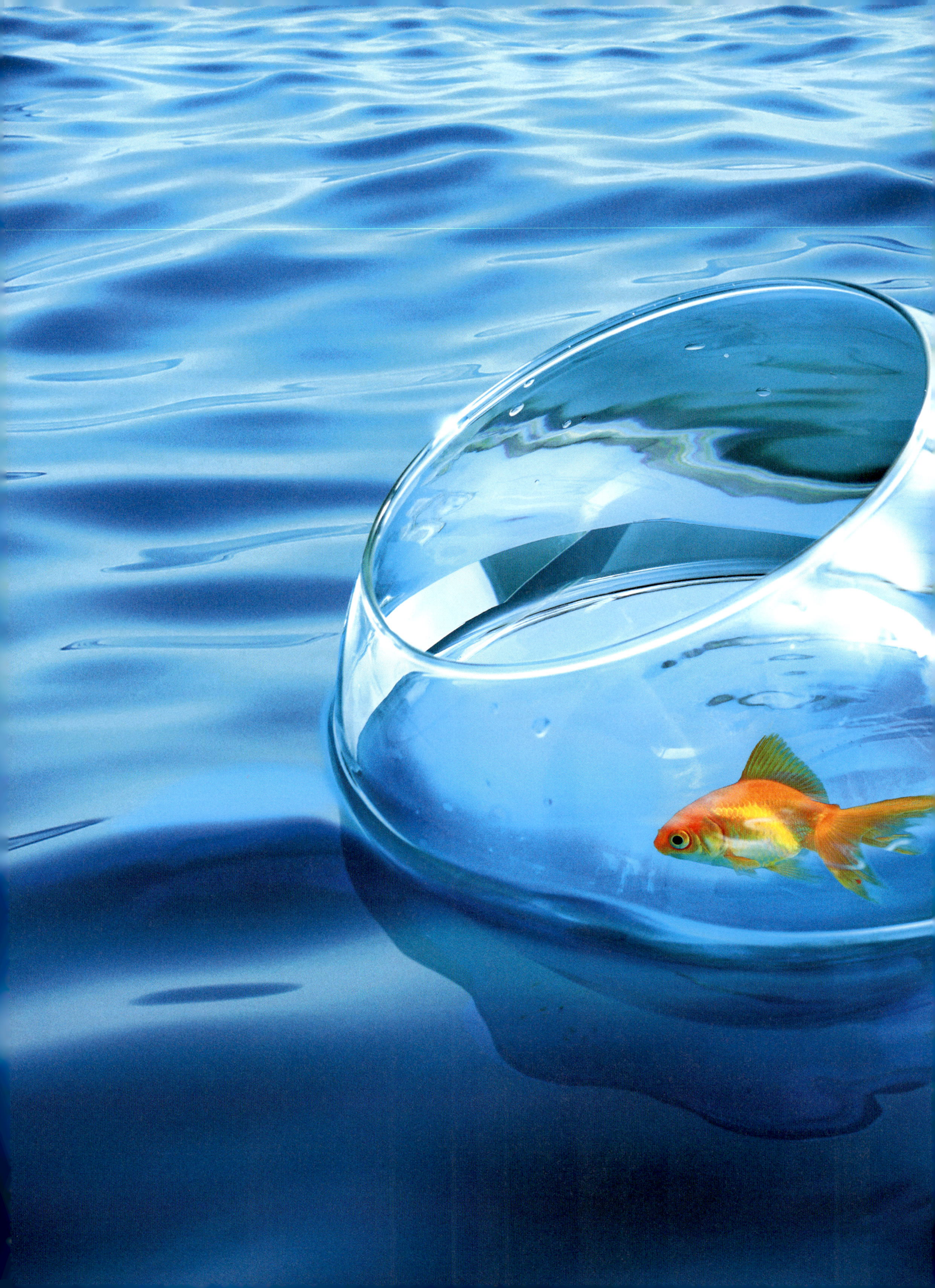

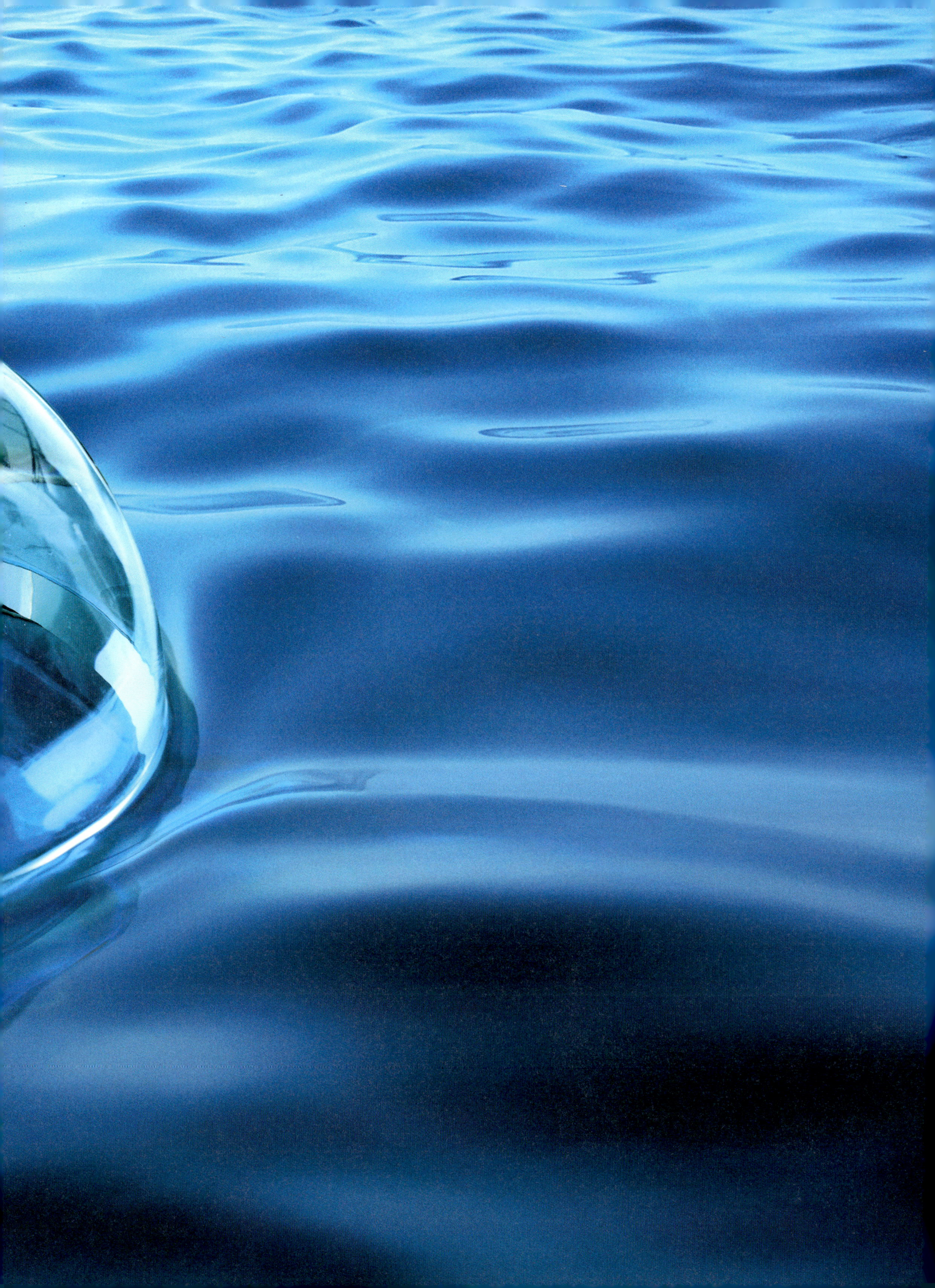

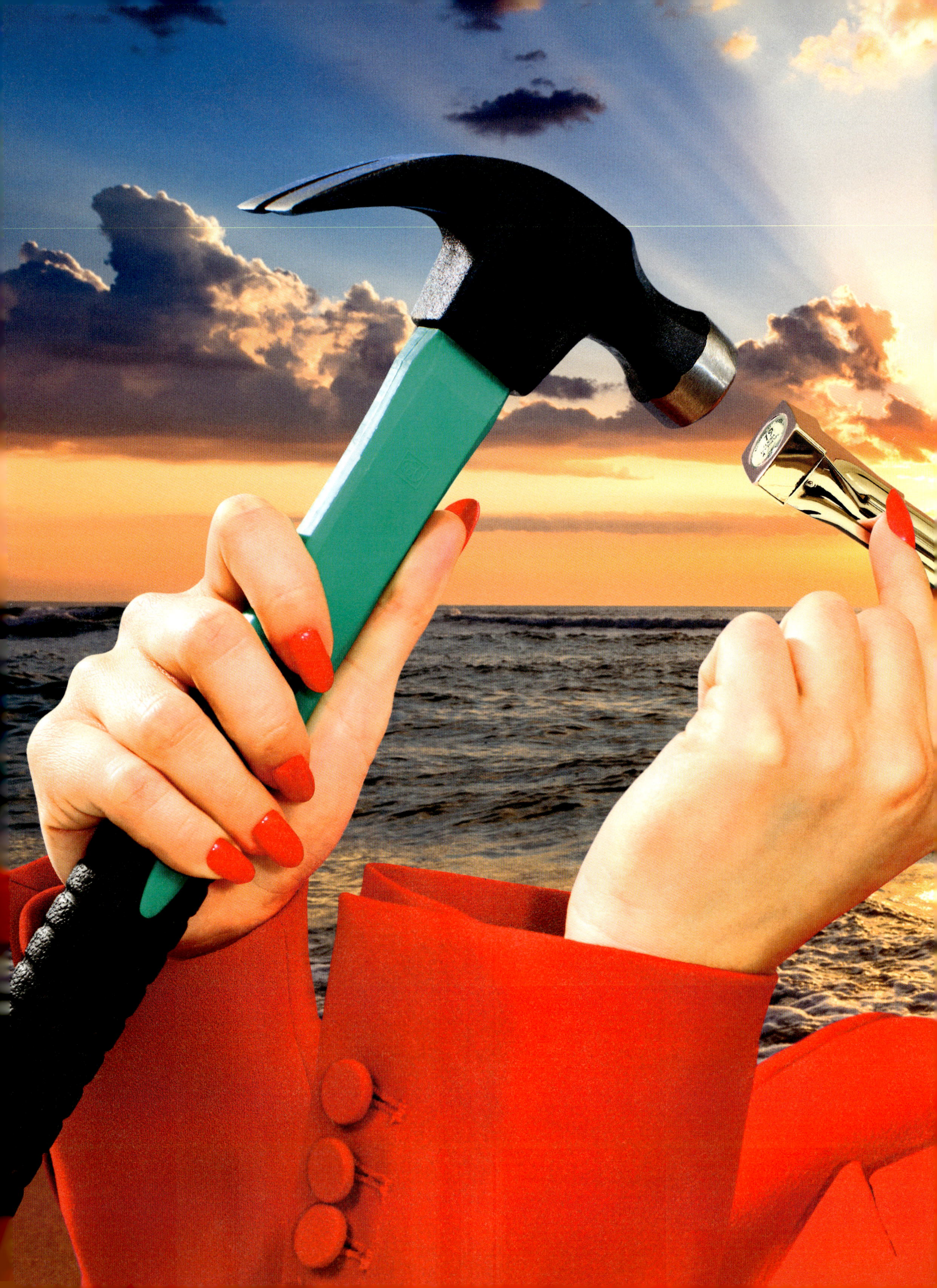

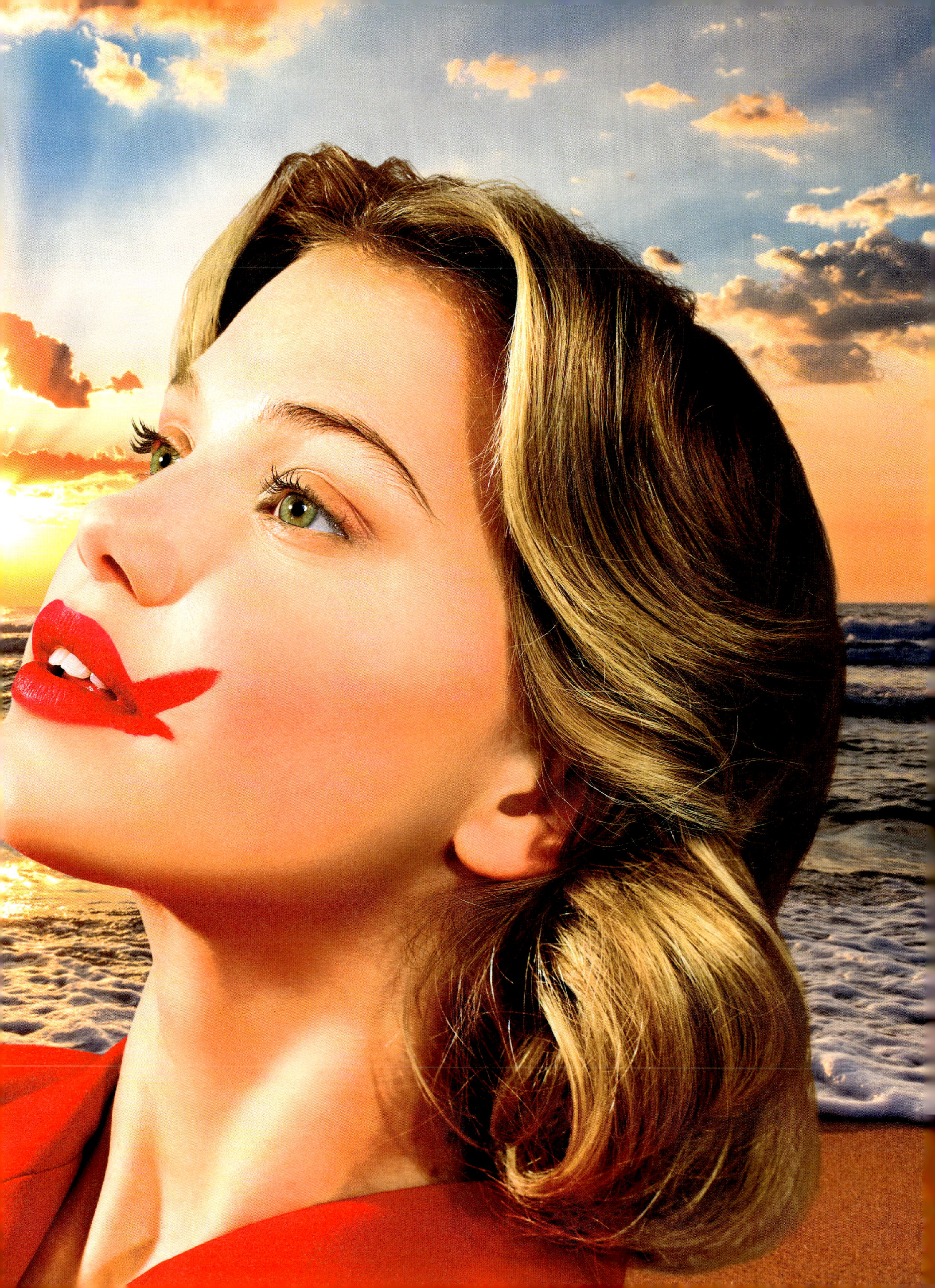

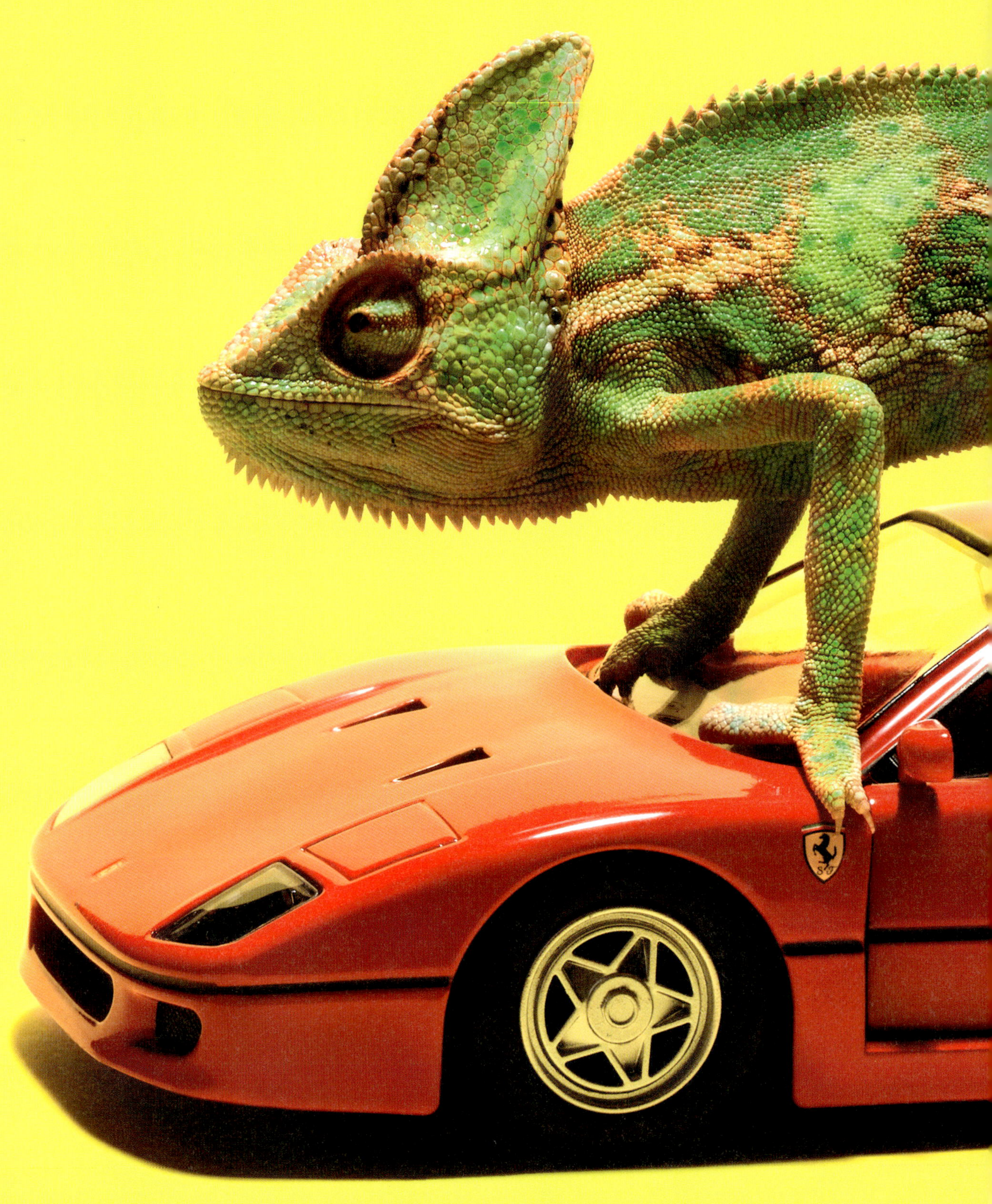